CHEAT CODE EXPLOSION

FOR CONSOLES

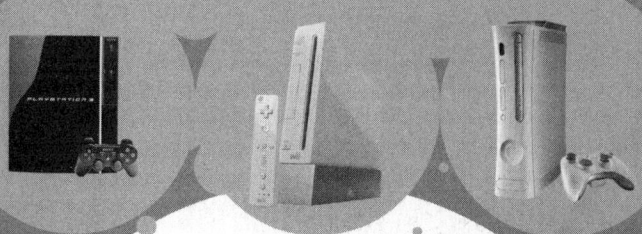

FLIP THIS BOOK OVER FOR HANDHELD SYSTEMS

Nintendo DS™

PlayStation® Portable

Game Boy® Advance

LOOK FOR CODEY

When you see Codey's face, you've found the newest and coolest codes!

SPECIAL SECTION: GUITAR HERO & ROCK BAND

GAMES LIST

GUITAR HERO

UNLOCK ALL

At the Main menu, press Yellow, Orange, Blue, Blue, Orange, Yellow, Yellow.

GUITAR HERO GUITAR CHEAT

At the Main menu, press Blue, Orange, Yellow, Blue, Blue.

CROWD METER CHEAT

At the Main menu, press Yellow, Blue, Orange, Orange, Blue, Blue, Yellow, Orange.

MONKEY HEAD CROWD CHEAT

At the Main menu, press Blue, Orange, Yellow, Yellow, Yellow, Blue, Orange.

SKULL HEAD CROWD CHEAT

At the Main menu, press Orange, Yellow, Blue, Blue, Orange, Yellow, Blue, Blue.

AIR GUITAR CHEAT

At the Main menu, press Orange, Orange, Blue, Yellow, Orange.

NO VENUE CHEAT

At the Main menu, press Blue, Yellow, Orange, Blue, Yellow, Orange.

GUITAR HERO II

AIR GUITAR

At the Main menu, press Yellow, Yellow, Blue, Orange, Yellow, Blue.

EYEBALL HEAD CROWD

At the Main menu, press Blue, Orange, Yellow, Orange, Yellow, Orange, Blue.

MONKEY HEAD CROWD

At the Main menu, press Orange, Blue, Yellow, Yellow, Orange, Blue, Yellow, Yellow.

FLAMING HEAD

At the Main menu, press Orange, Yellow, Orange, Orange, Yellow, Orange, Yellow, Yellow.

HORSE HEAD

At the Main menu, press Blue, Orange, Orange, Blue, Orange, Orange, Blue, Orange, Orange, Blue.

HYPER SPEED

At the Main menu, press Orange, Blue, Orange, Yellow, Orange, Blue, Orange, Yellow.

PERFORMANCE MODE

At the Main menu, press Yellow, Yellow, Blue, Yellow, Yellow, Orange, Yellow, Yellow.

GUITAR HERO III: LEGENDS OF ROCK

To enter the following cheats, strum the guitar while holding the listed buttons. For example, if the code lists Yellow + Orange, hold the Yellow and Orange buttons as you strum. Air Guitar, Precision Mode and Performance Mode can be toggled on and off from the Cheats menu. You can also change between five different levels of Hyperspeed at this menu.

UNLOCK EVERYTHING

Select Cheats from the Options. Choose Enter Cheat and enter the following (no sounds play while this code is entered):

Green + Red + Blue + Orange
Green + Red + Yellow + Blue
Green + Red + Yellow + Orange
Green + Yellow + Blue + Orange
Green + Red + Yellow + Blue
Red + Yellow + Blue + Orange
Green + Red + Yellow + Blue
Green + Yellow + Blue + Orange
Green + Red + Yellow + Blue
Green + Red + Yellow + Orange
Green + Red + Yellow + Orange
Green + Red + Yellow + Blue
Green + Red + Yellow + Orange

An easier way to illustrate this code is to represent Green as 1, progressing down the guitar neck to Orange as 5. For example, if you have 1345, you would hold Green + Yellow + Blue + Orange while strumming: 1245 + 1234 + 1235 + 1345 + 1234 + 2345 + 1234 + 1345 + 1234 + 1235 + 1235 + 1234 + 1235.

ALL SONGS

Select Cheats from the Options. Choose Enter Cheat and enter:

Yellow + Orange
Red + Blue
Red + Orange
Green + Blue
Red + Yellow
Yellow + Orange
Red + Yellow
Red + Blue
Green + Yellow
Green + Yellow
Yellow + Blue
Yellow + Blue
Yellow + Orange
Yellow + Orange
Yellow + Blue
Yellow
Red
Red + Yellow
Red
Yellow
Orange

NO FAIL

Select Cheats from the Options. Choose Enter Cheat and enter:

Green + Red
Blue
Green + Red
Green + Yellow
Blue
Green + Yellow
Red + Yellow
Orange
Red + Yellow
Green + Yellow
Yellow
Green + Yellow
Green + Red

AIR GUITAR

Select Cheats from the Options. Choose Enter Cheat and enter:

Blue + Yellow
Green + Yellow
Green + Yellow
Red + Blue
Red + Blue
Red + Yellow
Red + Yellow
Blue + Yellow
Green + Yellow
Green + Yellow
Red + Blue
Red + Blue
Red + Yellow
Red + Yellow
Green + Yellow
Green + Yellow
Red + Yellow
Red + Yellow

HYPERSPEED

Select Cheats from the Options. Choose Enter Cheat and enter:

Orange
Blue
Orange
Yellow
Orange
Blue
Orange
Yellow

PERFORMANCE MODE

Select Cheats from the Options. Choose Enter Cheat and enter:

Red + Yellow
Red + Blue
Red + Orange
Red + Blue
Red + Yellow
Green + Blue
Red + Yellow
Red + Blue

EASY EXPERT

Select Cheats from the Options. Choose Enter Cheat and enter:

Green + Red
Green + Yellow
Yellow + Blue
Red + Blue
Blue + Orange
Yellow + Orange
Red + Yellow
Red + Blue

PRECISION MODE

Select Cheats from the Options. Choose Enter Cheat and enter:

Green + Red
Green + Red
Green + Red
Red + Yellow
Red + Yellow
Red + Blue
Red + Blue
Yellow + Blue
Yellow + Orange
Yellow + Orange
Green + Red
Green + Red
Green + Red
Red + Yellow
Red + Yellow
Red + Blue
Red + Blue
Yellow + Blue
Yellow + Orange
Yellow + Orange

BRET MICHAELS SINGER

Select Cheats from the Options. Choose Enter Cheat and enter:

Green + Red
Green + Red
Green + Red
Green + Blue
Green + Blue
Green + Blue
Red + Blue
Red
Red
Red
Red + Blue
Red
Red
Red
Red + Blue
Red
Red
Red

GUITAR HERO ENCORE: ROCKS THE 80S

UNLOCK EVERYTHING

At the Main menu, press Blue, Orange, Yellow, Red, Orange, Yellow, Blue, Yellow, Red, Yellow, Blue, Yellow, Red, Yellow, Blue, Yellow.

HYPERSPEED

At the Main menu, press Yellow, Blue, Orange, Orange, Blue, Yellow, Yellow, Orange.

PERFORMANCE MODE

At the Main menu, press Blue, Blue, Orange, Yellow, Yellow, Blue, Orange, Blue.

AIR GUITAR

At the Main menu, press Yellow, Blue, Yellow, Orange, Blue, Blue.

EYEBALL HEAD CROWD

At the Main menu, press Yellow, Blue, Orange, Orange, Orange, Blue, Yellow.

MONKEY HEAD CROWD

At the Main menu, press Blue, Blue, Orange, Yellow, Blue, Blue, Orange, Yellow.

FLAME HEAD

At the Main menu, press Yellow, Orange, Yellow, Orange, Yellow, Orange, Blue, Orange.

HORSE HEAD

At the Main menu, press Blue, Orange, Orange, Blue, Yellow, Blue, Orange, Orange, Blue, Yellow.

GUITAR HERO: AEROSMITH

To enter the following cheats, strum the guitar while holding the listed buttons. For example, if the codes lists Yellow + Orange, hold Yellow and Orange as you strum. Air Guitar, Precision Mode, and Performance Mode can be toggled on and off from the Cheats menu. You can also change between five different levels of Hyperspeed at this menu.

ALL SONGS

Red + Yellow
Green + Red
Green + Red
Red + Yellow
Red + Yellow
Green + Red
Red + Yellow
Red + Yellow
Green + Red
Green + Red
Red + Yellow
Red + Yellow
Green + Red
Red + Yellow
Red + Blue

AIR GUITAR

Red + Yellow
Green + Red
Red + Yellow
Red + Yellow
Red + Blue
Red + Blue
Red + Blue
Red + Blue
Red + Blue
Yellow + Blue
Yellow + Blue
Yellow + Orange

HYPERSPEED

Yellow + Orange
Yellow + Orange
Yellow + Orange
Yellow + Orange
Yellow + Orange
Red + Yellow
Red + Yellow
Red + Yellow
Red + Yellow
Red + Blue
Red + Blue
Red + Blue
Red + Blue
Red + Blue
Yellow + Blue
Yellow + Orange
Yellow + Orange

NO FAIL

Green + Red
Blue
Green + Red
Green + Yellow
Blue
Green + Yellow
Red + Yellow
Orange
Red + Yellow
Green + Yellow
Yellow
Green + Yellow
Green + Red

PERFORMANCE MODE

Green + Red
Green + Red
Red + Orange
Red + Blue
Green + Red
Green + Red
Red + Orange
Red + Blue

PRECISION MODE

Red + Yellow
Red + Blue
Red + Blue
Red + Yellow
Red + Yellow
Yellow + Blue
Yellow + Blue
Yellow + Blue
Red + Blue
Red + Yellow
Red + Blue
Red + Blue
Red + Blue
Red + Yellow
Yellow + Blue
Yellow + Blue
Yellow + Blue
Red + Blue

GUITAR HERO WORLD TOUR

The following cheats can be toggled on and off at the Cheats menu.

QUICKPLAY SONGS

Select Cheats from the Options menu, choose Enter New Cheat and press Blue, Blue, Red, Green, Green, Blue, Blue, Yellow.

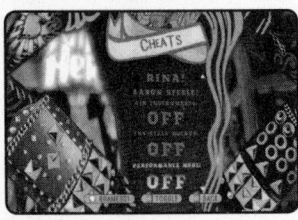 

ALWAYS SLIDE

Select Cheats from the Options menu, choose Enter New Cheat and press Green, Green, Red, Red, Yellow, Red, Yellow, Blue.

AT&T BALLPARK

Select Cheats from the Options menu, choose Enter New Cheat and press Yellow, Green, Red, Red, Green, Blue, Red, Yellow.

AUTO KICK

Select Cheats from the Options menu, choose Enter New Cheat and press Yellow, Green, Red, Blue (x4), Red.

EXTRA LINE 6 TONES

Select Cheats from the Options menu, choose Enter New Cheat and press Green, Red, Yellow, Blue, Red, Yellow, Blue, Green.

FLAME COLOR

Select Cheats from the Options menu, choose Enter New Cheat and press Green, Red, Green, Blue, Red, Red, Yellow, Blue.

GEM COLOR

Select Cheats from the Options menu, choose Enter New Cheat and press Blue, Red, Red, Green, Red, Green, Red, Yellow.

STAR COLOR

Select Cheats from the Options menu, choose Enter New Cheat and press Red, Red, Yellow, Red, Blue, Red, Red, Blue.

AIR INSTRUMENTS

Select Cheats from the Options menu, choose Enter New Cheat and press Red, Red, Blue, Yellow, Green (x3), Yellow.

HYPERSPEED

Select Cheats from the Options menu, choose Enter New Cheat and press Green, Blue, Red, Yellow, Yellow, Red, Green, Green. These show up in the menu as HyperGuitar, HyperBass, and HyperDrums.

PERFORMANCE MODE

Select Cheats from the Options menu, choose Enter New Cheat and press Yellow, Yellow, Blue, Red, Blue, Green, Red, Red.

INVISIBLE ROCKER

Select Cheats from the Options menu, choose Enter New Cheat and press Green, Red, Yellow (x3), Blue, Blue, Green.

VOCAL FIREBALL

Select Cheats from the Options menu, choose Enter New Cheat and press Red, Green, Green, Yellow, Blue, Green, Yellow, Green.

AARON STEELE!

Select Cheats from the Options menu, choose Enter New Cheat and press Blue, Red, Yellow (x5), Green.

JONNY VIPER

Select Cheats from the Options menu, choose Enter New Cheat and press Blue, Red, Blue, Blue, Yellow (x3), Green.

NICK

Select Cheats from the Options menu, choose Enter New Cheat and press Green, Red, Blue, Green, Red, Blue, Blue, Green.

RINA

Select Cheats from the Options menu, choose Enter New Cheat and press Blue, Red, Green, Green, Yellow (x3), Green.

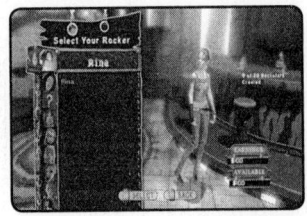

GUITAR HERO 5

ALL HOPOS

Select Input Cheats from the Options menu and enter Green, Green, Blue, Green, Green, Green, Yellow, Green.

ALWAYS SLIDE

Select Input Cheats from the Options menu and enter Green, Green, Red, Red, Yellow, Blue, Yellow, Blue.

AUTO KICK

Select Input Cheats from the Options menu and enter Yellow, Green, Red, Blue, Blue, Blue, Blue, Red.

FOCUS MODE

Select Input Cheats from the Options menu and enter Yellow, Green, Red, Green, Yellow, Blue, Green, Green.

HUD FREE MODE

Select Input Cheats from the Options menu and enter Green, Red, Green, Green, Yellow, Green, Green, Green.

PERFORMANCE MODE

Select Input Cheats from the Options menu and enter Yellow, Yellow, Blue, Red, Blue, Green, Red, Red.

AIR INSTRUMENTS

Select Input Cheats from the Options menu and enter Red, Red, Blue, Yellow, Green, Green, Green, Yellow.

INVISIBLE ROCKER

Select Input Cheats from the Options menu and enter Green, Red, Yellow, Yellow, Yellow, Blue, Blue, Green.

ALL CHARACTERS

Select Input Cheats from the Options menu and enter Blue, Blue, Green, Green, Red, Green, Red, Yellow.

CONTEST WINNER 1

Select Input Cheats from the Options menu and enter Green, Green, Red, Red, Yellow, Red, Yellow, Blue.

GUITAR HERO: METALLICA

Once entered, the cheats must be activated in the Cheats menu.

METALLICA COSTUMES

Select Cheats from Settings and enter Green, Red, Yellow, Blue, Blue, Yellow, Red, Green.

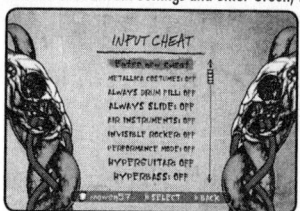 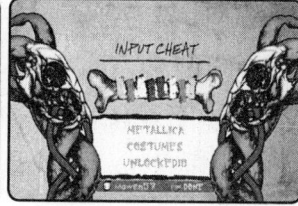

HYPERSPEED

Select Cheats from Settings and enter Green, Blue, Red, Yellow, Yellow, Red, Green, Green.

PERFORMANCE MODE

Select Cheats from Settings and enter Yellow, Yellow, Blue, Red, Blue, Green, Red, Red.

INVISIBLE ROCKER

Select Cheats from Settings and enter Green, Red, Yellow (x3), Blue, Blue, Green.

AIR INSTRUMENTS

Select Cheats from Settings and enter Red, Red, Blue, Yellow, Green (x3), Yellow.

ALWAYS DRUM FILL

Select Cheats from Settings and enter Red (x3), Blue, Blue, Green, Green, Yellow.

AUTO KICK

Select Cheats from Settings and enter Yellow, Green, Red, Blue (x4), Red. With this cheat activated, the bass pedal is automatically hit.

ALWAYS SLIDE

Select Cheats from Settings and enter Green, Green, Red, Red, Yellow, Red, Yellow, Blue. All Guitar Notes Become Touch Pad Sliding Notes.

BLACK HIGHWAY

Select Cheats from Settings and enter Yellow, Red, Green, Red, Green, Red, Red, Blue.

FLAME COLOR

Select Cheats from Settings and enter Green, Red, Green, Blue, Red, Red, Yellow, Blue.

GEM COLOR

Select Cheats from Settings and enter Blue, Red, Red, Green, Red, Green, Red, Yellow.

STAR COLOR

Select Cheats from Settings and enter Press Red, Red, Yellow, Red, Blue, Red, Red, Blue.

ADDITIONAL LINE 6 TONES

Select Cheats from Settings and enter Green, Red, Yellow, Blue, Red, Yellow, Blue, Green.

VOCAL FIREBALL

Select Cheats from Settings and enter Red, Green, Green, Yellow, Blue, Green, Yellow, Green.

GUITAR HERO: SMASH HITS

Enter the following in the cheats menu which can be found in the options menu.

ALWAYS DRUM FILL

Green, Green, Red, Red, Blue, Blue, Yellow, Yellow

ALWAYS SLIDE

Blue, Yellow, Red, Green, Blue, Green, Green, Yellow

HYPERSPEED

Red, Green, Blue, Yellow, Green, Yellow, Red, Red

AIR INSTRUMENTS

Yellow, Red, Blue, Green, Yellow, Red, Red, Red

INVISIBLE ROCKER

Blue, Red, Red, Red, Red, Yellow, Blue, Green

GEM COLOR

Red, Red, Red, Blue, Blue, Blue, Yellow, Green

STAR COLOR

Green, Red, Green, Yellow, Green, Blue, Yellow, Red

LINE 6 UNLOCK
Green, Red, Yellow, Blue, Red, Yellow, Blue, Green

VOCAL FIREBALL
Green, Blue, Red, Red, Yellow, Yellow, Blue, Blue

ROCK BAND

ALL SONGS
At the title screen, press Red, Yellow, Blue, Red, Red, Blue, Blue, Red, Yellow, Blue. Saving and all network features are disabled with this code.

TRANSPARENT INSTRUMENTS
Complete the hall of fame concert with that instrument.

GOLD INSTRUMENT
Complete the solo tour with that instrument.

SILVER INSTRUMENT
Complete the bonus tour with that instrument.

ROCK BAND 2

Most of these codes disable saving, achievements, and Xbox LIVE play.

UNLOCK ALL SONGS
Select Modify Game from the Extras menu, choose Enter Unlock Code and press Red, Yellow, Blue, Red, Red, Blue, Blue, Red, Yellow, Blue or Y, B, X, Y, Y, X, X, Y, B, X. Toggle this cheat on or off from the Modify Game menu.

SELECT VENUE SCREEN

Select Modify Game from the Extras menu, choose Enter Unlock Code and press Blue, Orange, Orange, Blue, Yellow, Blue, Orange, Orange, Blue, Yellow or (for Xbox 360) X, Left Bumper, Left Bumper, X, B, X, Left Bumper, Left Bumper, X, B. Toggle this cheat on or off from the Modify Game menu.

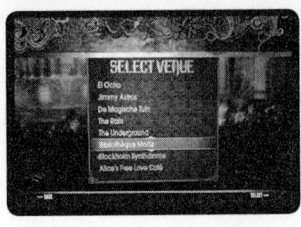

NEW VENUES ONLY

Select Modify Game from the Extras menu, choose Enter Unlock Code and press Red, Red, Red, Red, Yellow, Yellow, Yellow, Yellow or (for Xbox 360) Y (x4), B (x4). Toggle this cheat on or off from the Modify Game menu.

PLAY THE GAME WITHOUT A TRACK

Select Modify Game from the Extras menu, choose Enter Unlock Code and press Blue, Blue, Red, Red, Yellow, Yellow, Blue, Blue or (for Xbox 360) X, X, Y, Y, B, B, X, X. Toggle this cheat on or off from the Modify Game menu.

AWESOMENESS DETECTION

Select Modify Game from the Extras menu, choose Enter Unlock Code and press Yellow, Blue, Orange, Yellow, Blue, Orange, Yellow, Blue, Orange or (for Xbox 360) B, X, Left Bumper, B, X, Left Bumper, B, X, Left Bumper. Toggle this cheat on or off from the Modify Game menu.

STAGE MODE

Select Modify Game from the Extras menu, choose Enter Unlock Code and press Blue, Yellow, Red, Blue, Yellow, Red, Blue, Yellow, Red or (for Xbox 360) X, B, Y, X, B, Y, X, B, Y. Toggle this cheat on or off from the Modify Game menu.

THE BEATLES: ROCK BAND

BONUS PHOTOS

At the title screen, press Blue, Yellow, Orange, Orange, Orange, Blue, Blue, Blue, Yellow, Orange.

PLAYSTATION® 3

CONTENTS

BAJA: EDGE OF CONTROL

CAREER COMPLETE 100%

Select Cheat Codes from the Options menu and enter SHOWTIME.

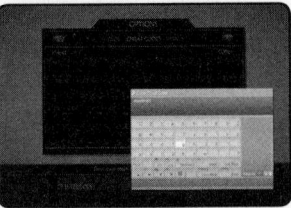 

INSTALL ALL PARTS

Select Cheat Codes from the Options menu and enter SUPERMAX.

BEJEWELED 2

TOGGLE CLASSIC STYLE GEMS

During a game, hold L1 + L2 + R1 + R2 and press ✕.

TOGGLE GAME BORDERS

During a game, hold L1 + L2 + R1 + R2 and press ⬤.

THE BIGS

START A ROOKIE WITH HIGHER STATS

When you create a rookie, name him HOT DOG. His stats will be higher than when you normally start.

BLAZING ANGELS 2: SECRET MISSIONS OF WWII

ALL MISSIONS AND PLANES UNLOCKED

At the main menu, hold L2 + R2, and press ⬤, L1, R1, ⬤, ⬤, R1, L1, ⬤.

GOD MODE

Pause the game, hold L2, and press ⬤, ⬤, ⬤, ⬤. Release L2, hold R2 and press ⬤, ⬤, ⬤, ⬤. Re-enter the code to disable it.

INCREASED DAMAGE WITH ALL WEAPONS

Pause the game, hold L2, and press L1, L1, R1. Release L2, hold R2, and press R1, R1, L1. Re-enter the code to disable it.

BOLT

Many of the following cheats can be toggled on/off by pausing the game and selecting Cheats.

LEVEL SELECT

Select Cheats from the Extras menu and enter Right, Up, Left, Right, Up, Right.

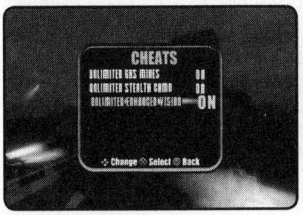 

ALL MINIGAMES

Select Cheats from the Extras menu and enter Right, Up, Right, Right.

UNLIMITED ENHANCED VISION

Select Cheats from the Extras menu and enter Left, Right, Up, Down.

UNLIMITED GROUND POUND

Select Cheats from the Extras menu and enter Right, Up, Right, Up, Left, Down.

UNLIMITED INVULNERABILITY

Select Cheats from the Extras menu and enter Down, Down, Up, Left.

UNLIMITED GAS MINES

Select Cheats from the Extras menu and enter Right, Left, Left, Up, Down, Right.

UNLIMITED LASER EYES

Select Cheats from the Extras menu and enter Left, Left, Up, Right.

UNLIMITED STEALTH CAMO

Select Cheats from the Extras menu and enter Left, Down (x3).

UNLIMITED SUPERBARK

Select Cheats from the Extras menu and enter Right, Left, Left, Up, Down, Up.

BURNOUT PARADISE

BEST BUY CAR

Pause the game and select Sponsor Product Code from the Under the Hood menu. Enter Bestbuy. Need A License to use this car offline.

CIRCUIT CITY CAR

Pause the game and select Sponsor Product Code from the Under the Hood menu. Enter Circuitcity. Need Burnout Paradise License to use this car offline.

GAMESTOP CAR

Pause the game and select Sponsor Product Code from the Under the Hood menu. Enter Gamestop. Need A License to use this car offline.

WALMART CAR

Pause the game and select Sponsor Product Code from the Under the Hood menu.. Enter Walmart. Need Burnout Paradise License to use this car offline.

"STEEL WHEELS" GT

Pause the game and select Sponsor Product Code from the Under the Hood menu. Enter G23X 5K8Q GX2V 04B1 or E60J 8Z7T MS8L 51U6.

LICENSES

LICENSE	NUMBER OF WINS NEEDED
D	2
C	7
B	16
A	26
Burnout Paradise	45
Elite License	All events

CARS MATER-NATIONAL

ALL ARCADE RACES, MINI-GAMES, AND WORLDS

Select Codes/Cheats from the options and enter PLAYALL.

ALL CARS

Select Codes/Cheats from the options and enter MATTEL07.

ALTERNATE LIGHTNING MCQUEEN COLORS

Select Codes/Cheats from the options and enter NCEDUDZ.

ALL COLORS FOR OTHERS

Select Codes/Cheats from the options and enter PAINTIT.

UNLIMITED TURBO

Select Codes/Cheats from the options and enter ZZOOOOM.

EXTREME ACCELERATION

Select Codes/Cheats from the options and enter 0TO200X.

EXPERT MODE

Select Codes/Cheats from the options and enter VRYFAST.

ALL BONUS ART

Select Codes/Cheats from the options and enter BUYTALL.

DIRT 2

Win the given events to earn the following cars:

GET THIS CAR	BY WINNING THIS EVENT
Ford RS200 Evolution	Rally Cross World Tour
Toyota Stadium Truck	Landrush World Tour
Mitsubishi Pajero Dakar 1993	Raid World Tour
Dallenbach Special	Trailblazer World Tour
1995 Subaru Impreza WRX STi	Colin McRae Challenge
Colin McRae R4 [X Games]	X Games Europe
Mitsubishi Lancer Evolution X [X Games]	X Games Asia
Subaru Impreza WRX STi [X Games]	X Games America
Ford Escort MKII and MG Metro 6R4	All X Games events

G.I. JOE: THE RISE OF COBRA

CLASSIC DUKE

At the main menu, press Left, Up, ⬤, Up, Right, ▲.

SHANA "SCARLETT" O'HARA

At the main menu, press Right, Up, Down, Down, ▲.

GRID

ALL DRIFT CARS

Select Bonus Codes from the Options. Then choose Enter Code and enter TUN58396.

ALL MUSCLE CARS

Select Bonus Codes from the Options. Then choose Enter Code and enter MUS59279.

BUCHBINDER EMOTIONAL ENGINEERING BMW 320SI

Select Bonus Codes from the Options. Then choose Enter Code and enter F93857372. You can use this in Race Day or in GRID World once you've started your own team.

EBAY MOTORS MUSTANG

Select Bonus Codes from the Options. Then choose Enter Code and enter DAFJ55E01473M0. You can use this in Race Day or in GRID World once you've started your own team.

GAMESTATION BMW 320SI

Select Bonus Codes from the Options. Then choose Enter Code and enter G29782655. You can use this in Race Day or in GRID World once you've started your own team.

MICROMANIA PAGANI ZONDA R

Select Bonus Codes from the Options. Then choose Enter Code and enter M38572343. You can use this in Race Day or in GRID World once you've started your own team.

PLAY.COM ASTON MARTIN DBR9

Select Bonus Codes from the Options. Then choose Enter Code and enter P47203845. You can use this in Race Day or in GRID World once you've started your own team.

IRON MAN

CLASSIC ARMOR

Clear One Man Army vs. Mercs.

EXTREMIS ARMOR

Clear One Man Army vs. Maggia.

MARK II ARMOR

Clear One Man Army vs. Ten Rings.

HULKBUSTER ARMOR

Clear One Man Army vs. AIM-X. Can also be unlocked when clear game save data from Incredible Hulk is stored on the same console.

CLASSIC MARK I ARMOR

Clear One Man Army vs. AIM.

ULTIMATE ARMOR

Clear Mission 13: Showdown.

PLAYSTATION® 3

CHEAT CODE EXPLOSION FOR CONSOLES

JUICED 2: HOT IMPORT NIGHTS

ASCARI KZ1
Select Cheats and Codes from the DNA Lab menu and enter KNOX. Defeat the challenge to earn the car.

AUDI TT 1.8L QUATTRO
Select Cheats and Codes from the DNA Lab menu and enter YTHZ. Defeat the challenge to earn the car.

BMW Z4 ROADSTER
Select Cheats and Codes from the DNA Lab menu and enter GVDL. Defeat the challenge to earn the car.

FRITO-LAY INFINITI G35
Select Cheats and Codes from the DNA Lab menu and enter MNCH. Defeat the challenge to earn the car.

HOLDEN MONARO
Select Cheats and Codes from the DNA Lab menu and enter RBSG. Defeat the challenge to earn the car.

HYUNDAI COUPE 2.7L V6
Select Cheats and Codes from the DNA Lab menu and enter BSLU. Defeat the challenge to earn the car.

INFINITI G35
Select Cheats and Codes from the DNA Lab menu and enter MRHC. Defeat the challenge to earn the car.

KOENIGSEGG CCX
Select Cheats and Codes from the DNA Lab menu and enter KDTR. Defeat the challenge to earn the car.

MITSUBISHI PROTOTYPE X
Select Cheats and Codes from the DNA Lab menu and enter DOPX. Defeat the challenge to earn the car.

NISSAN 350Z
Select Cheats and Codes from the DNA Lab menu and enter PRGN. Defeat the challenge to earn the car.

NISSAN SKYLINE R34 GT-R
Select Cheats and Codes from the DNA Lab menu and enter JWRS. Defeat the challenge to earn the car.

SALEEN S7
Select Cheats and Codes from the DNA Lab menu and enter WIKF. Defeat the challenge to earn the car.

SEAT LEON CUPRA R
Select Cheats and Codes from the DNA Lab menu and enter FAMQ. Defeat the challenge to earn the car.

KUNG FU PANDA

UNLIMITED CHI
Select Cheats from the Extra menu and enter Down, Right, Left, Up, Down.

INVULNERABILITY
Select Cheats from the Extra menu and enter Down, Down, Right, Up, Left.

FULL UPGRADES
Select Cheats from the Extra menu and enter Left, Right, Down, Left, Up.

FULL AWESOME METER
Select Cheats from the Extra menu and enter Up, Down, Up, Right, Left. This gives Po 4X damage.

MULTIPLAYER CHARACTERS
Select Cheats from the Extra menu and enter Left, Down, Left, Right, Down.

OUTFITS
Select Cheats from the Extra menu and enter Right, Left, Down, Up, Right.

 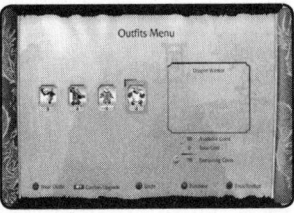

LAIR

CHICKEN VIDEO
At the cheat menu, enter chicken.

COFFEE VIDEO
At the cheat menu, enter 686F7420636F66666565.

UNLOCKS STABLE OPTION FOR ALL LEVELS
At the cheat menu, enter koelsch. Saving is disabled with this code.

THE LEGEND OF SPYRO: DAWN OF THE DRAGON

UNLIMITED LIFE
Pause the game, hold L1 and press Right, Right, Down, Down, Left with the Left Analog Stick.

UNLIMITED MANA
Pause the game, hold R1 and press Up, Right, Up, Left, Down with the Left Analog Stick.

MAXIMUM XP
Pause the game, hold R1 and press Left, Right, Right, Up, Up with the Left Analog Stick.

ALL ELEMENTAL UPGRADES
Pause the game, hold L1 and press Left, Up, Down, Up, Right with the Left Analog Stick.

LEGO BATMAN

BATCAVE CODES
Using the computer in the Batcave, select Enter Code and enter the following codes.

 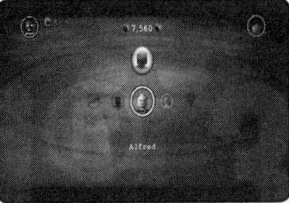

CHARACTERS

CHARACTER	CODE	CHARACTER	CODE
Alfred	ZAQ637	Penguin Henchman	BJH782
Batgirl	JKR331	Penguin Minion	KJP748
Bruce Wayne	BDJ327	Poison Ivy Goon	GTB899
Catwoman (Classic)	M1AAWW	Police Marksman	HKG984
Clown Goon	HJK327	Police Officer	JRY983
Commissioner Gordon	DDP967	Riddler Goon	CRY928
Fishmonger	HGY748	Riddler Henchman	XEU824
Freeze Girl	XVK541	S.W.A.T.	HTF114
Joker Goon	UTF782	Sailor	NAV592
Joker Henchman	YUN924	Scientist	JFL786
Mad Hatter	JCA283	Security Guard	PLB946
Man-Bat	NYU942	The Joker (Tropical)	CCB199
Military Policeman	MKL382	Yeti	NJL412
Nightwing	MVY759	Zoo Sweeper	DWR243
Penguin Goon	NKA238		

VEHICLES

VEHICLE	CODE	VEHICLE	CODE
Bat-Tank	KNTT4B	Mr. Freeze's Kart	BCT229
Bruce Wayne's Private Jet	LEA664	Penguin Goon Submarine	BTN248
Catwoman's Motorcycle	HPL826	Police Bike	LJP234
Garbage Truck	DUS483	Police Boat	PLC999
Goon Helicopter	GCH328	Police Car	KJL832
Harbor Helicopter	CHP735	Police Helicopter	CWR732
Harley Quinn's Hammer Truck	RDT637	Police Van	MAC788
Mad Hatter's Glider	HS000W	Police Watercraft	VJD328
Mad Hatter's Steamboat	M4DM4N	Riddler's Jet	HAHAHA
Mr. Freeze's Iceberg	ICYICE	Robin's Submarine	TTF453
The Joker's Van	JUK657	Two-Face's Armored Truck	EFE933

CHEATS

CHEAT	CODE	CHEAT	CODE
Always Score Multiply	9LRGNB	More Batarang Targets	XWP645
Fast Batarangs	JRBDCB	Piece Detector	KHJ554
Fast Walk	ZOLM6N	Power Brick Detector	MMN786
Flame Batarang	D8NYWH	Regenerate Hearts	HJH7HJ
Freeze Batarang	XPN4NG	Score x2	N4NR3E
Extra Hearts	ML3KHP	Score x4	CX9MAT
Fast Build	EVG26J	Score x6	MLVNF2
Immune to Freeze	JXUDY6	Score x8	WCCDB9
Invincibility	WYD5CP	Score x10	18HW07
Minikit Detector	ZXGH9J		

LEGO INDIANA JONES: THE ORIGINAL ADVENTURES

CHARACTERS

Approach the blackboard in the Classsroom and enter the following codes.

CHARACTER	CODE	CHARACTER	CODE
Bandit	12N68W	Fedora	V75YSP
Bandit Swordsman	1MK4RT	First Mate	0GIN24
Barranca	04EM94	Grail Knight	NE6THI
Bazooka Trooper (Crusade)	MK83R7	Hovitos Tribesman	H0V1SS
Bazooka Trooper (Raiders)	S93Y5R	Indiana Jones (Desert Disguise)	4J8S4M
Belloq	CHN3YU	Indiana Jones (Officer)	VJ850S
Belloq (Jungle)	TDR197	Jungle Guide	24PF34
Belloq (Robes)	VEO29L	Kao Kan	WMO46L
British Commander	B73EUA	Kazim	NRH23J
British Officer	VJ5TI9	Kazim (Desert)	3M29TJ
British Soldier	DJ5I2W	Lao Che	2NK479
Captain Katanga	VJ3TT3	Maharajah	NFK5N2
Chatter Lal	ENW936	Major Toht	13NS01
Chatter Lal (Thuggee)	CNH4RY	Masked Bandit	N48SFO
Chen	3NK48T	Mola Ram	FJUR31
Colonel Dietrich	2K9RKS	Monkey Man	3RF6YJ
Colonel Vogel	8EAL4H	Pankot Assassin	2NKT72
Dancing Girl	C7EJ21	Pankot Guard	VN28RH
Donovan	3NFTU8	Sherpa Brawler	VJ37WJ
Elsa (Desert)	JSNRT9	Sherpa Gunner	ND762W
Elsa (Officer)	VMJ5US	Slave Child	0E3ENW
Enemy Boxer	8246RB	Thuggee	VM683E
Enemy Butler	VJ48W3	Thuggee Acolyte	T2R3F9
Enemy Guard	VJ7R51	Thuggee Slave Driver	VBS7GW
Enemy Guard (Mountains)	YR47WM	Village Dignitary	KD48TN
Enemy Officer	572E61	Village Elder	4682E1
Enemy Officer (Desert	2MK450	Willie (Dinner Suit)	VK93R7
Enemy Pilot	B84ELP	Willie (Pajamas)	MEN4IP
Enemy Radio Operator	1MF94R	Wu Han	3NSLT8
Enemy Soldier (Desert)	4NSU7Q		

EXTRAS

Approach the blackboard in the Classsroom and enter the following codes. Some cheats need to be enabled by selecting Extras from the pause menu.

CHEAT	CODE	CHEAT	CODE
Artifact Detector	VIKED7	Regenerate Hearts	MDLP69
Beep Beep	VNF59Q	Secret Characters	3X44AA
Character Treasure	VIES2R	Silhouettes	3HE85H
Disarm Enemies	VKRNS9	Super Scream	VN3R7S
Disguises	4ID1N6	Super Slap	0P1TA5
Fast Build	V83SLO	Treasure Magnet	H86LA2
Fast Dig	378RS6	Treasure x10	VI3PS8
Fast Fix	FJ59WS	Treasure x2	VM4TS9
Fertilizer	B1GW1F	Treasure x4	VLWEN3
Ice Rink	33GM7J	Treasure x6	V84RYS
Parcel Detector	VUT673	Treasure x8	A72E1M
Poo Treasure	WWQ1SA		

LEGO STAR WARS: THE COMPLETE SAGA

The following still need to be purchase after entering the codes.

CHARACTERS

ADMIRAL ACKBAR

At the bar in Mos Eisley Cantina, select Enter Code and enter ACK646.

BATTLE DROID (COMMANDER)

At the bar in Mos Eisley Cantina, select Enter Code and enter KPF958.

BOBA FETT (BOY)

At the bar in Mos Eisley Cantina, select Enter Code and enter GGF539.

BOSS NASS

At the bar in Mos Eisley Cantina, select Enter Code and enter HHY697.

CAPTAIN TARPALS

At the bar in Mos Eisley Cantina, select Enter Code and enter QRN714.

COUNT DOOKU

At the bar in Mos Eisley Cantina, select Enter Code and enter DDD748.

DARTH MAUL

At the bar in Mos Eisley Cantina, select Enter Code and enter EUK421.

EWOK

At the bar in Mos Eisley Cantina, select Enter Code and enter EWK785.

GENERAL GRIEVOUS

At the bar in Mos Eisley Cantina, select Enter Code and enter PMN576.

GREEDO

At the bar in Mos Eisley Cantina, select Enter Code and enter ZZR636.

IG-88

At the bar in Mos Eisley Cantina, select Enter Code and enter GIJ989.

IMPERIAL GUARD

At the bar in Mos Eisley Cantina, select Enter Code and enter GUA850.

JANGO FETT

At the bar in Mos Eisley Cantina, select Enter Code and enter KLJ897.

KI-ADI MUNDI

At the bar in Mos Eisley Cantina, select Enter Code and enter MUN486.

LUMINARA

At the bar in Mos Eisley Cantina, select Enter Code and enter LUM521.

PADMÉ

At the bar in Mos Eisley Cantina, select Enter Code and enter VBJ322.

R2-Q5

At the bar in Mos Eisley Cantina, select Enter Code and enter EVILR2.

STORMTROOPER

At the bar in Mos Eisley Cantina, select Enter Code and enter NBN431.

TAUN WE

At the bar in Mos Eisley Cantina, select Enter Code and enter PRX482.

VULTURE DROID
At the bar in Mos Eisley Cantina, select Enter Code and enter BDC866.

WATTO
At the bar in Mos Eisley Cantina, select Enter Code and enter PLL967.

ZAM WESELL
At the bar in Mos Eisley Cantina, select Enter Code and enter 584HJF.

SKILLS

DISGUISE
At the bar in Mos Eisley Cantina, select Enter Code and enter BRJ437.

FORCE GRAPPLE LEAP
At the bar in Mos Eisley Cantina, select Enter Code and enter CLZ738.

VEHICLES

DROID TRIFIGHTER
At the bar in Mos Eisley Cantina, select Enter Code and enter AAB123.

IMPERIAL SHUTTLE
At the bar in Mos Eisley Cantina, select Enter Code and enter HUT845.

TIE INTERCEPTOR
At the bar in Mos Eisley Cantina, select Enter Code and enter INT729.

TIE FIGHTER
At the bar in Mos Eisley Cantina, select Enter Code and enter DBH897.

ZAM'S AIRSPEEDER
At the bar in Mos Eisley Cantina, select Enter Code and enter UUU875.

MARVEL ULTIMATE ALLIANCE

UNLOCK ALL SKINS
At the Team Menu, press Up, Down, Left, Right, Left, Right, Start.

UNLOCKS ALL HERO POWERS
At the Team Menu, press Left, Right, Up, Down, Up, Down, Start.

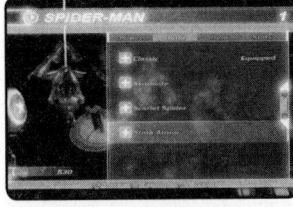 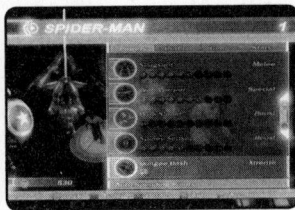

ALL HEROES TO LEVEL 99
At the Team Menu, press Up, Left, Up, Left, Down, Right, Down, Right, Start.

UNLOCK ALL HEROES
At the Team Menu, press Up, Up, Down, Down, Left, Left, Left, Start.

UNLOCK DAREDEVIL

At the Team Menu, press Left, Left, Right, Right, Up, Down, Up, Down, Start.

UNLOCK SILVER SURFER

At the Team Menu, press Down, Left, Left, Up, Right, Up, Down, Left, Start.

GOD MODE

During gameplay, press Up, Down, Up, Down, Up, Left, Down, Right, Start.

TOUCH OF DEATH

During gameplay, press Left, Right, Down, Down, Right, Left, Start.

SUPER SPEED

During gameplay, press Up, Left, Up, Right, Down, Right, Start.

FILL MOMENTUM

During gameplay, press Left, Right, Right, Left, Up, Down, Down, Up, Start.

UNLOCK ALL COMICS

At the Review menu, press Left, Right, Right, Left, Up, Up, Right, Start.

UNLOCK ALL CONCEPT ART

At the Review menu, press Down, Down, Down, Right, Right, Left, Down, Start.

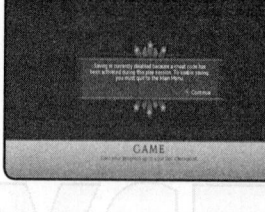

UNLOCK ALL CINEMATICS

At the Review menu, press Up, Left, Left, Up, Right, Right, Up, Start.

UNLOCK ALL LOAD SCREENS

At the Review menu, press Up, Down, Right, Left, Up, Up Down, Start.

UNLOCK ALL COURSES

At the Comic Missions menu, press Up, Right, Left, Down, Up, Right, Left, Down, Start.

MARVEL: ULTIMATE ALLIANCE 2

These codes will disable the ability to save.

GOD MODE

During a game, press Up, Down, Up, Down, Up, Left, Down, Right, Start.

UNLIMITED FUSION

During a game, press Right, Right, Up, Down, Up, Up, Left, Start.

UNLOCK ALL POWERS

During a game, press Left, Right, Up, Down, Up, Down, Start.

UNLOCK ALL HEROES

During a game, press Up, Up, Down, Down, Left, Left, Left, Start.

UNLOCK ALL SKINS

During a game, press Up, Down, Left, Right, Left, Right, Start.

UNLOCK JEAN GREY

During a game, press Left, Left, Right, Right, Up, Down, Up, Down, Start.

UNLOCK HULK

During a game, press Down, Left, Left, Up, Right, Up, Down, Left, Start.

UNLOCK THOR

During a game, press Up, Right, Right, Down, Right, Down, Left, Right, Start.

UNLOCK ALL AUDIO LOGS

At the main menu, press Left, Right, Right, Left, Up, Up, Right, Start.

UNLOCK ALL DOSSIERS

At the main menu, press Down, Down, Down, Right, Right, Left, Down, Start.

UNLOCK ALL MOVIES

At the main menu, press Up, Left, Left, Up, Right, Right, Up, Start.

MLB 07: THE SHOW

CLASSIC STADIUMS

At the Main Menu, press Down, Up, Right, Down, Up, Left, Down, Up.

GOLDEN/SLIVER ERA PLAYERS

At the Main Menu, press Left, Up, Right, Down, Down, Left, Up, Down.

MLB 08: THE SHOW

ALL CLASSIC STADIUMS

At the main menu, press Down, Right, Circle, Square, Left, Triangle, Up, L1. The controller will vibrate if entered correctly.

MX VS. ATV UNTAMED

ALL RIDING GEAR

Select Cheat Codes from the Options and enter crazylikea.

ALL HANDLEBARS

Select Cheat Codes from the Options and enter nohands.

NASCAR 08

ALL CHASE MODE CARS

Select cheat codes from the options menu and enter checkered flag.

EA SPORTS CAR

Select cheat codes from the options menu and enter ea sports car.

FANTASY DRIVERS

Select cheat codes from the options menu and enter race the pack.

WALMART CAR AND TRACK

Select cheat codes from the options menu and enter walmart everyday.

NASCAR 09

WAL-MART CAR & CHICAGO PIER RACETRACK

Select EA Extras from My Nascar, then choose Cheat Codes and enter WALMART EVERYDAY.

NBA 09: THE INSIDE

EASTERN ALL-STARS 09 JERSEY

Select Extras from the Progression menu. Then choose nba.com from the Jerseys menu. Press ● and enter SHPNV2K699.

WESTERN ALL-STARS 09 JERSEY

Select Extras from the Progression menu. Then choose nba.com from the Jerseys menu. Press ● and enter K8AV6YMLNF.

L.A. LAKERS LATIN NIGHT JERSEY

Select Extras from the Progression menu. Then choose nba.com from the Jerseys menu. Press ● and enter NMTWCTC84S.

MIAMI HEAT LATIN NIGHT JERSEY

Select Extras from the Progression menu. Then choose nba.com from the Jerseys menu. Press ● and enter WCTGSA8SPD.

PHOENIX SUNS LATIN NIGHT JERSEY

Select Extras from the Progression menu. Then choose nba.com from the Jerseys menu. Press ● and enter LKUTSENFJH.

SAN ANTONIO SPURS LATIN NIGHT JERSEY

Select Extras from the Progression menu. Then choose nba.com from the Jerseys menu. Press ● and enter JFHSY73MYD.

NBA 2K8

ABA BALL

Select Codes from the Features menu and enter Payrespect.

2KSPORTS TEAM

Select Codes from the Features menu and enter 2ksports.

NBA DEVELOPMENT TEAM

Select Codes from the Features menu and enter nba2k.

SUPERSTARS TEAM

Select Codes from the Features menu and enter llmohffaae.

VISUAL CONCEPTS TEAM

Select Codes from the Features menu and enter Vcteam.

2008 ALL-STAR NBA JERSEYS

Select Codes from the Features menu and enter haeitgyebs.

BOBCATS RACING JERSEY
Select Codes from the Features menu and enter agtaccsinr.

PACERS SECOND ROAD JERSEY
Select Codes from the Features menu and enter cpares.

ST. PATRICK'S DAY JERSEYS
Select Codes from the Features menu and enter uclerehanp.

VALENTINE'S DAY JERSEYS
Select Codes from the Features menu and enter amcnreo.

NBA 2K9

2K SPORTS TEAM
Select Codes from the Features menu and enter 2ksports.

NBA 2K TEAM
Select Codes from the Features menu and enter nba2k.

SUPERSTARS
Select Codes from the Features menu and enter llmohffaae.

VC TEAM
Select Codes from the Features menu and enter vcteam.

ABA BALL
Select Codes from the Features menu and enter payrespect.

NBA 2K10

ABA BALL
Select Codes from Options and enter payrespect.

2K CHINA TEAM
Select Codes from Options and enter 2kchina.

NBA 2K TEAM
Select Codes from Options and enter nba2k.

2K SPORTS TEAM
Select Codes from Options and enter 2ksports.

VISUAL CONCEPTS TEAM
Select Codes from Options and enter vcteam.

NBA LIVE 07

AIR JORDAN V

Select NBA Codes from My NBA Live 07 and enter PNBBX1EVT5.

AIR JORDAN V

Select NBA Codes from My NBA Live 07 and enter VIR13PC451.

AIR JORDAN V

Select NBA Codes from My NBA Live 07 and enter IB7G8NN91Z.

JORDAN MELO M3

Select NBA Codes from My NBA Live 07 and enter JUL38TC485.

C-BILLUPS ALL-STAR EDITION

Select NBA Codes from My NBA Live 07 and enter BV6877HB9N.

ADIDAS C-BILLUPS VEGAS EDITION

Select NBA Codes from My NBA Live 07 and enter 85NVLDMWS5.

ADIDAS GARNETT BOUNCE ALL-STAR EDITION

Select NBA Codes from My NBA Live 07 and enter HYIOUHCAAN.

ADIDAS GARNETT BOUNCE VEGAS EDITION

Select NBA Codes from My NBA Live 07 and enter KDZ2MQL17W.

ADIDAS GIL-ZERO ALL-STAR EDITION

Select NBA Codes from My NBA Live 07 and enter 23DN1PPOG4.

ADIDAS GIL-ZERO VEGAS EDITION

Select NBA Codes from My NBA Live 07 and enter QQQ3JCUYQ7.

ADIDAS GIL-ZERO MID

Select NBA Codes from My NBA Live 07 and enter 1GSJC8JWRL.

ADIDAS GIL-ZERO MID

Select NBA Codes from My NBA Live 07 and enter 369V6RVU3G.

ADIDAS STEALTH ALL-STAR EDITION

Select NBA Codes from My NBA Live 07 and enter FE454DFJCC.

ADIDAS T-MAC 6 ALL-STAR EDITION

Select NBA Codes from My NBA Live 07 and enter MCJK843NNC.

ADIDAS T-MAC 6 VEGAS EDITION

Select NBA Codes from My NBA Live 07 and enter 84GF7EJG8V.

CHARLOTTE BOBCATS SECOND ROAD JERSEY

Select NBA Codes from My NBA Live 07 and enter WEDX671H7S.

UTAH JAZZ SECOND ROAD JERSEY

Select NBA Codes from My NBA Live 07 and enter VCBI89FK83.

NEW JERSEY NETS SECOND ROAD JERSEY

Select NBA Codes from My NBA Live 07 and enter D4SAA98U5H.

WASHINGTON WIZARDS SECOND ROAD JERSEY

Select NBA Codes from My NBA Live 07 and enter QV93NLKXQC.

EASTERN ALL-STARS 2007 ROAD JERSEY

Select NBA Codes from My NBA Live 07 and enter WOCNW4KL7L.

EASTERN ALL-STARS 2007 HOME JERSEY
Select NBA Codes from My NBA Live 07 and enter 5654ND43N6.

WESTERN ALL-STARS 2007 ROAD JERSEY
Select NBA Codes from My NBA Live 07 and enter XX93BVL20U.

WESTERN ALL-STARS 2007 HOME JERSEY
Select NBA Codes from My NBA Live 07 and enter 993NSKL199.

NBA LIVE 08

ADIDAS GIL-ZERO – ALL-STAR EDITION
Select NBA Codes from My NBA and enter 23DN1PPOG4.

ADIDAS TIM DUNCAN STEALTH – ALL-STAR EDITION
Select NBA Codes from My NBA and enter FE454DFJCC.

NBA LIVE 09

SUPER DUNKS MODE
Use the Sprite vending machine in the practice area and enter spriteslam.

 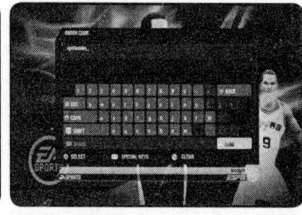

NBA STREET HOMECOURT

ALL TEAMS
At the Main menu, hold **R1** + **L1** and press Left, Right, Left, Right.

ALL COURTS
At the Main menu, hold **R1** + **L1** and press Up, Right, Down, Left.

BLACK/RED BALL
At the Main menu, hold **R1** + **L1** and press Up, Down, Left, Right.

NEED FOR SPEED PROSTREET

$2,000
Select Career and then choose Code Entry. Enter 1MA9X99.

$4,000

Select Career and then choose Code Entry. Enter W2IOLL01.

$8,000

Select Career and then choose Code Entry. Enter L1IS97A1.

$10,000

Select Career and then choose Code Entry. Enter 1MI9K7E1.

$10,000

Select Career and then choose Code Entry. Enter CASHMONEY.

$10,000

Select Career and then choose Code Entry. Enter REGGAME.

AUDI TT

Select Career and then choose Code Entry. Enter ITSABOUTYOU.

CHEVELLE SS

Select Career and then choose Code Entry. Enter HORSEPOWER.

COKE ZERO GOLF GTI

Select Career and then choose Code Entry. Enter COKEZERO.

DODGE VIPER

Select Career and then choose Code Entry. Enter WORLDSLONGESTLASTING.

MITSUBISHI LANCER EVOLUTION

Select Career and then choose Code Entry. Enter MITSUBISHIGOFAR.

UNLOCK ALL BONUSES

Select Career and then choose Code Entry. Enter UNLOCKALLTHINGS.

5 REPAIR MARKERS

Select Career and then choose Code Entry. Enter SAFETYNET.

ENERGIZER VINYL

Select Career and then choose Code Entry. Enter ENERGIZERLITHIUM.

CASTROL SYNTEC VINYL

Select Career and then choose Code Entry. Enter CASTROLSYNTEC. This also gives you $10,000.

NEED FOR SPEED UNDERCOVER

$10,000

Select Secret Codes from the Options menu and enter %%S3/".

DIE-CAST BMW M3 E92

Select Secret Codes from the Options menu and enter)B7@B=.

DIE-CAST LEXUS IS F

Select Secret Codes from the Options menu and enter 0;5M2;.

NEEDFORSPEED.COM LOTUS ELISE

Select Secret Codes from the Options menu and enter -KJ3=E.

DIE-CAST NISSAN 240SX (S13)

Select Secret Codes from the Options menu and enter ?P:COL.

DIE-CAST PORSCHE 911 TURBO

Select Secret Codes from the Options menu and enter >8P:I;.

SHELBY TERLINGUA
Select Secret Codes from the Options menu and enter NeedForSpeedShelbyTerlingua.

DIE-CAST VOLKSWAGEN R32
Select Secret Codes from the Options menu and enter!2ODBJ:.

NHL 08

ALL RBK EDGE JERSEYS
At the RBK Edge Code option, enter h3oyxpwksf8ibcgt.

NHL 2K9

3RD JERSEYS
From the Features menu, enter R6y34bsH52 as a code.

PRINCE OF PERSIA

SANDS OF TIME PRINCE/FARAH SKINS
Select Skin Manager from the Extras menu. Press ⬤ and enter 52585854. This gives you the Sands of Time skin for the Prince and Farah from Sands of Time for the Princess. Access them from the Skin Manager

PRINCE ALTAIR IBN LA-AHAD SKIN
Create an Ubisoft account. Then select "Altair Skin for Prince" to unlock.

RATATOUILLE

Select Gusteau's Shop from the Extras menu. Choose Secrets, select the appropriate code number, and then enter the code. Once the code is entered, select the cheat you want to activate it.

CODE NUMBER	CODE	EFFECT
1	Pieceocake	Very Easy difficulty mode
2	Myhero	no impact and no damage from enemies
3	Shielded	No damage from enemies
4	Spyagent	Move undetected by any enemy
5	Ilikeonions	Fart every time Remy jumps
6	Hardfeelings	Head butt when attacking instead of tailswipe
7	Slumberparty	Multiplayer mode
8	Gusteauart	All Concept Art
9	Gusteauship	All four championship modes
10	Mattelme	All single player and multiplayer minigames
11	Gusteauvid	All Videos
12	Gusteaures	All Bonus Artworks
13	Gusteaudream	All Dream Worlds in Gusteau's Shop
14	Gusteauslide	All Slides in Gusteau's Shop
15	Gusteaulevel	All single player minigames
16	Gusteaucombo	All items in Gusteau's Shop
17	Gusteaupot	5,000 Gusteau points
18	Gusteaujack	10,000 Gusteau points
19	Gusteauomni	50,000 Gusteau points

RATCHET & CLANK FUTURE: TOOLS OF DESTRUCTION

CHALLENGE MODE

After defeating the game, you can replay the game in Challenge Mode with all of Ratchet's current upgraded weapons and armor.

SKILL POINTS

Complete the following objectives to earn skill points. Each one is worth 10 to 40 points and you can use these points to unlock Cheats in the Cheats Menu. The following table lists the skill points with a location and description.

SKILL POINT	LOCATION	DESCRIPTION
Smashing Good Time	Cobalia	Destroy all crates and consumer bots in the trade port and gel factory.
I Should Have Gone Down in a Barrel	Cobalia	Jump into each of the two gel waterfall areas in Cobalia gel factory.
Giant Hunter	Cobalia	Kill several Basilisk Leviathans in the Cobalia wilderness.
Wrench Ninja 3	Stratus City	Use only the Omniwrench to get through the level to the Robo-Wings segment.
We Don't Need No Stinkin' Bridges!	Stratus City	Cross the tri-pad sequence using gel-cube bounces.
Surface-to-Air Plasma Beasts	Stratus City	Take out several flying targets using a specific weapon.
Been Around	Stratus City	Take off from every Robo-wing launch pad in Stratus City.
Collector's Addition	Voron	Be very thorough in your collection of goodies.
Minesweeper	Voron	Clear out a bunch of mines.
What's That, R2?	Voron	Barrel roll multiple times.
I Think I'm Gonna Be Sick	IFF	Ride the Ferris wheel for 5 loops without getting off or taking damage.
Fast and the Fire-ious	IFF	Use the Charge Boots to cross the bridge to the arena without being burned.
One Heckuva Peephole	IFF	Return after receiving the Geo-laser and complete the Geo-laser setup.
Alphabet City	Apogee	Teleport to each of the six asteroids in alphabetical order.
Knock You Down to Size	Apogee	Wrench Slam 5 centipedes.
Dancin' with the Stars	Apogee	Make 5 enemies dance at once on an asteroid.
Taste o' Yer Own Medicine	Pirate Base	Destroy all of the Shooter Pirates with the Combuster.
Preemptive Strike	Pirate Base	Destroy all of the "sleeping bats" while they are still sleeping.
It's Mutant-E Cap'n!	Pirate Base	Change 5 pirates into penguins in one blast.
You Sunk My Battleship!	Rakar	Shoot down a large percentage of the big destroyers.
Pretty Lights	Rakar	Complete the level without destroying any of the snatchers that fire beams at Ratchet.
I've Got Places To Be	Rakar	Destroy the boss in under 2:30.
The Consumer Is Not (Always) Right	Rykan V	Destroy a bunch of consumer bots in the level.
Live Strong	Rykan V	Complete the Gryo Cycle in 1:45.
Untouchable	Rykan V	Don't take damage in the Gyro-Cycle.
It Sounded Like a Freight Train	Sargasso	Get 10 Swarmers in one tornado.
Head Examiner	Sargasso	Land on each of the dinosaur heads in Sargasso.
Extinction	Sargasso	Kill all of the Sargasso Predators.
Lombaxes Don't Like Cold	Iris	Break all the breakable icicles.
Mow Down Ho-Down	Iris	Use turrets to destroy 10 dancing pirates.
Dancin' on the Ceiling	Zordoom	Successfully use a Groovitron while on a Magboot surface.

SKILL POINT	LOCATION	DESCRIPTION
Seared Ahi	Zordoom	Use the Pyroblaster on 3 Drophid creatures after freeing them from their robotic suits.
Shocking Ascent	Zordoom	Destroy all enemies on the elevator using just the Shock Ravager.
Expert Marksman	Borag	Kill 75% of all of the enemies.
Can't Touch This	Borag	Don't take damage before fighting the boss.
Pyoo, Pyoo!	Borag	Complete the level without secondary fire.
Dead Aim	Kerchu	Destroy several destructible towers while on the pirate barge.
Fire With Fire	Kerchu	Kill a few Kerchu Flamethrowers with the Pyro Blaster.
Rocket Jump	Kerchu	Successfully jump over a row of three rockets while on the grindrail during the boss fight in Kerchu City.
Your Friendly Neighborhood...	Slag Fleet	Destroy 5 enemies while on the grav ramp before Slag's ship.
Turret Times Two	Slag Fleet	Destroy at least 2 pirates with each turret in the level.
Six Gun Salute	Slag Fleet	Get six pirates in a row to salute Ratchet while in the Pirate Disguise.
Gotta Catch 'Em All	Cragmite Ruins	Hit all Cragmite soldiers with the Mag-Net Launcher.
Ratchet and Goliath	Cragmite Ruins	Destroy multiple walkers using just the Nano-Swarmers.
Ratchet &...Not Clank?!	Cragmite Ruins	Use Mr. Zurkon in Cragmite's Ratchet-only segment.
Stay Still So I Can Shoot You!	Meridian	Use strafe-flip 10 times while fighting the Cragmite soldiers.
Now Boarding...	Meridian	Complete the Gyro-Cycle in 55 seconds.
Low Flying Howls	Meridian	Fly under an electrified barrier in the Robo-wings segment.
Extreme Alien Makeover	Fastoon2	Turn 10 Cragmites into penguins.
Empty Bag o' Tricks	Fastoon2	Complete the level without using any devices.
Nowhere to Hide	Fastoon2	Destroy every piece of breakable cover.
No, Up Your Arsenal	Global	Upgrade every weapon to the max.
Roflcopter	Global	Turn enemies into penguins, then use the Visicopter to destroy the penguins.
Stir Fry	Global	Kill 2 different enemy types using the Shock Ravager while they are trapped in a tornado.
Golden Children	Overall	Find all of the Gold Bolts.
Sacagawea	Global	Complete all of the maps 100%, leaving no area undiscovered.
Cheapskate	Global	Purchase a single Combustor round.
Everybody Dance Now	Global	Make every type of enemy in the game dance.
F5 on the Fujita Scale	Global	Pick up more than 10 enemies with one tornado.
Chorus line	Global	Get 10+ enemies to dance together.
Happy Feet	Global	Get several penguins to dance on-screen.
Disco Inferno	Global	Use the Groovitron followed by the Pyro Blaster.
Bolts in the Bank	Global	Sell a bunch of Leviathan Souls to the Smuggler.
It's Like the North Pole Here	Global	Have at least 12-15 enemies and/or citizens turned into penguins at one time.
Say Hello to My Little Friend	Global	Kill 15 enemies with one RYNO shot.
For the Hoard!	Global	Get every item.
Promoted to Inspector	Global	Get every gadget.
Global Thermonuclear War	Global	Get every weapon.
It's Even Better the Second Time!	Global	Complete Challenge Mode.
The Hardest of Core	Global	Get all skill points and everything else in the game.

ROCK REVOLUTION

ALL CHARACTERS

At the main menu, press ●, ■, ●, ■, ●, ■, ●, ▲, ■.

ALL VENUES

At the main menu, press ■, ●, ▲, ●, ■, ●, ▲, ■, ▲.

SEGA SUPERSTARS TENNIS

UNLOCK CHARACTERS

Complete the following missions to unlock the corresponding character.

CHARACTER	MISSION TO COMPLETE
Alex Kidd	Mission 1 of Alex Kidd's World
Amy Rose	Mission 2 of Sonic the Hedgehog's World
Gilius	Mission 1 of Golden Axe's World
Gum	Mission 12 of Jet Grind Radio's World
Meemee	Mission 8 of Super Monkey Ball's World
Pudding	Mission 1 of Space Channel 5's World
Reala	Mission 2 of NiGHTs' World
Shadow The Hedgehog	Mission 14 of Sonic the Hedgehog's World

THE SIMPSONS GAME

After unlocking the following, the outfits can be changed at the downstairs closet in the Simpson's house. The Trophies can be viewed at different locations in the house: Bart's room, Lisa's room, Marge's room, and the garage.

BART'S OUTFITS AND TROPHIES (POSTER COLLECTION)

At the main menu, press Right, Left, ■, ■, ▲, R3.

HOMER'S OUTFITS AND TROPHIES (BEER BOTTLE COLLECTION)

At the main menu, press Left, Right, ▲, ▲, ■, L3.

LISA'S OUTFITS AND TROPHIES (DOLLS)

At the main menu, press ■, ▲, ■, ■, ■, Triangle, L3.

MARGE'S OUTFITS AND TROPHIES (HAIR PRODUCTS)

At the main menu, press ▲, ■, ▲, ▲, ■, R3.

SKATE

BEST BUY CLOTHES

At the Main menu, press Up, Down, Left, Right, ■, R1, ▲, L1.

SKATE 2

BIG BLACK

Select Enter Cheat from the Extras menu and enter letsdowork.

3D MODE

Select Enter Cheat from the Extras menu and enter strangeloops. Use glasses to view in 3D.

36

STAR WARS: THE FORCE UNLEASHED

CHEAT CODES

Pause the game and select Input Code. Here you can enter the following codes. Activating any of the following cheat codes will disable some unlockables, and you will be unable to save your progress.

CHEAT	CODE
All Force Powers at Max Power	KATARN
All Force Push Ranks	EXARKUN
All Saber Throw Ranks	ADEGAN
All Repulse Ranks	DATHOMIR
All Saber Crystals	HURRIKANE
All Talents	JOCASTA
Deadly Saber	LIGHTSABER

COMBOS

Pause the game and select Input Code. Here you can enter the following codes. Activating any of the following cheat codes will disable some unlockables, and you will be unable to save your progress.

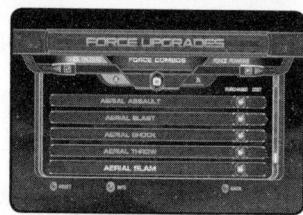

COMBO	CODE
All Combos	MOLDYCROW
Aerial Ambush	VENTRESS
Aerial Assault	EETHKOTH
Aerial Blast	YADDLE
Impale	BRUTALSTAB
Lightning Bomb	MASSASSI
Lightning Grenade	RAGNOS
Saber Slam	PLOKOON
Saber Sling	KITFISTO
Sith Saber Flurry	LUMIYA
Sith Slash	DARAGON
Sith Throw	SAZEN
New Combo	FREEDON
New Combo	MARAJADE

ALL DATABANK ENTRIES

Pause the game and select Input Code. Enter OSSUS.

MIRRORED LEVEL

Pause the game and select Input Code. Enter MINDTRICK. Re-enter the code to return level to normal.

SITH MASTER DIFFICULTY

Pause the game and select Input Code. Enter SITHSPAWN.

COSTUMES

Pause the game and select Input Code. Here you can enter the following codes.

COSTUME	CODE
All Costumes	SOHNDANN
Bail Organa	VICEROY
Ceremonial Jedi Robes	DANTOOINE
Drunken Kota	HARDBOILED
Emperor	MASTERMIND
Incinerator Trooper	PHOENIX
Jedi Adventure Robe	HOLOCRON
Kashyyyk Trooper	TK421GREEN
Kota	MANDALORE
Master Kento	WOOKIEE
Proxy	PROTOTYPE
Scout Trooper	FERRAL
Shadow Trooper	BLACKHOLE
Sith Stalker Armor	KORRIBAN
Snowtrooper	SNOWMAN
Stormtrooper	TK421WHITE
Stormtrooper Commander	TK421BLUE

STAR WARS THE CLONE WARS: REPUBLIC HEROES

SPIDER DROID-JAK UPGRADE

Pause the game, select Cheats from the Shop, and press Up, Left, Down, Left, Right, Left, Left Left.

STUNTMAN IGNITION

3 PROPS IN STUNT CREATOR MODE

Select Cheats from Extras and enter COOLPROP.

ALL ITEMS UNLOCKED FOR CONSTRUCTION MODE

Select Cheats from Extras and enter NOBLEMAN.

MVX SPARTAN

Select Cheats from Extras and enter fastride.

ALL CHEATS

Select Cheats from Extras and enter Wearefrozen.

This unlocks the following cheats: Slo-mo Cool, Thrill Cam, Vision Switcher, Nitro Addiction, Freaky Fast, and Ice Wheels.

ALL CHEATS

Select Cheats from Extras and enter Kungfoopete.

ICE WHEELS CHEAT

Select Cheats from Extras and enter IceAge.

NITRO ADDICTION CHEAT

Select Cheats from Extras and enter TheDuke.

VISION SWITCHER CHEAT

Select Cheats from Extras and enter GFXMODES.

SUPER PUZZLE FIGHTER II TURBO HD REMIX

PLAY AS AKUMA

At the character select, highlight Hsien-Ko and press Down.

PLAY AS DAN

At the character select, highlight Donovan and press Down.

PLAY AS DEVILOT

At the character select, highlight Morrigan and press Down.

PLAY AS ANITA

At the character select, hold **L1** + **R1** and choose Donovan.

PLAY AS HSIEN-KO'S TALISMAN

At the character select, hold **L1** + **R1** and choose Hsien-Ko.

PLAY AS MORRIGAN AS A BAT

At the character select, hold **L1** + **R1** and choose Morrigan.

SURF'S UP

ALL CHAMPIONSHIP LOCATIONS

Select Cheat Codes from the Extras menu and enter FREEVISIT.

ALL LEAF SLIDE STAGES

Select Cheat Codes from the Extras menu and enter GOINGDOWN.

ALL MULTIPLAYER LEVELS

Select Cheat Codes from the Extras menu and enter MULTIPASS.

ALL BOARDS

Select Cheat Codes from the Extras menu and enter MYPRECIOUS.

ASTRAL BOARD

Select Cheat Codes from the Extras menu and enter ASTRAL.

MONSOON BOARD

Select Cheat Codes from the Extras menu and enter MONSOON.

TINE SHOCKWAVE BOARD

Select Cheat Codes from the Extras menu and enter TINYSHOCKWAVE.

ALL CHARACTER CUSTOMIZATIONS

Select Cheat Codes from the Extras menu and enter TOPFASHION.

PLAY AS ARNOLD

Select Cheat Codes from the Extras menu and enter TINYBUTSTRONG.

PLAY AS ELLIOT

Select Cheat Codes from the Extras menu and enter SURPRISEGUEST.

PLAY AS GEEK

Select Cheat Codes from the Extras menu and enter SLOWANDSTEADY.

PLAY AS TANK EVANS

Select Cheat Codes from the Extras menu and enter IMTHEBEST.

PLAY AS TATSUHI KOBAYASHI

Select Cheat Codes from the Extras menu and enter KOBAYASHI.

PLAY AS ZEKE TOPANGA

Select Cheat Codes from the Extras menu and enter THELEGEND.

ALL VIDEOS AND SPEN GALLERY

Select Cheat Codes from the Extras menu and enter WATCHAMOVIE.

ART GALLERY

Select Cheat Codes from the Extras menu and enter NICEPLACE.

TIGER WOODS PGA TOUR 08

ALL COURSES

Select Password from EA Sports Extras
and enter greensfees.

ALL GOLFERS

Select Password from EA Sports Extras and enter allstars.

WAYNE ROONEY

Select Password from EA Sports Extras
and enter playfifa08.

INFINITE MONEY

Select Password from EA Sports Extras and enter cream.

TOM CLANCY'S HAWX

A-12 AVENGER II

At the hangar, hold L2 and press ●, L1, ●, R1, ▲, ●.

F-18 HARV

At the hangar, hold L2 and press L1, ▲, L1, ▲, L1, ●.

FB-22 STRIKE RAPTOR

At the hangar, hold L2 and press R1, ●, R1, ●, R1, ▲.

TONY HAWK'S PROVING GROUND

Select Cheat Codes from the Options and enter the following cheats. Some codes need to be enabled by selecting Cheats from the Options during a game.

UNLOCK	CHEAT
Unlocks Boneman	CRAZYBONEMAN
Unlocks Bosco	MOREMILK
Unlocks Cam	NOTACAMERA
Unlocks Cooper	THECOOP
Unlocks Eddie X	SKETCHY
Unlocks El Patinador	PILEDRIVER
Unlocks Eric	FLYAWAY
Unlocks Mad Dog	RABBIES
Unlocks MCA	INTERGALACTIC
Unlocks Mel	NOTADUDE
Unlocks Rube	LOOKSSMELLY
Unlocks Spence	DAPPER
Unlocks Shayne	MOVERS
Unlocks TV Producer	SHAKER

UNLOCK	CHEAT
Unlock FDR	THEPREZPARK
Unlock Lansdowne	THELOCALPARK
Unlock Air & Space Museum	THEINDOORPARK
Unlocks all Fun Items	OVERTHETOP
Unlocks all CAS items	GIVEMESTUFF
Unlocks all Decks	LETSGOSKATE
Unlock all Game Movies	WATCHTHIS
Unlock all Lounge Bling Items	SWEETSTUFF
Unlock all Lounge Themes	LAIDBACKLOUNGE
Unlock all Rigger Pieces	IMGONNABUILD
Unlock all Video Editor Effects	TRIPPY
Unlock all Video Editor Overlays	PUTEMONTOP

UNLOCK	CHEAT
All specials unlocked and in player's special list	LOTSOFTRICKS
Full Stats	BEEFEDUP

UNLOCK	CHEAT
Give player +50 skill points	NEEDSHELP

The following cheats lock you out of the Leaderboards:

UNLOCK	CHEAT
Unlocks Perfect Manual	STILLAINTFALLIN
Unlocks Perfect Rail	AINTFALLIN
Unlock Super Check	BOOYAH
Unlocks Unlimited Focus	MYOPIC
Unlock Unlimited Slash Grind	SUPERSLASHIN

UNLOCK	CHEAT
Unlocks 100% branch completion in NTT	FOREVERNAILED
No Bails	ANDAINTFALLI

You can not use the Video Editor with the following cheats:

UNLOCK	CHEAT
Unlocks Invisible Man	THEMISSING
Mini Skater	TINYTATER
No Board	MAGICMAN

TRANSFORMERS: THE GAME

INFINITE HEALTH
At the Main menu, press Left, Left, Up, Left, Right, Down, Right.

INFINITE AMMO
At the Main menu, press Up, Down, Left, Right, Up, Up, Down.

NO MILITARY OR POLICE
At the Main menu, press Right, Left, Right, Left, Right, Left, Right.

ALL MISSIONS
At the Main menu, press Down, Up, Left, Right, Right, Right, Up, Down.

BONUS CYBERTRON MISSIONS
At the Main menu, press Right, Up, Up, Down, Right, Left, Left.

GENERATION 1 SKIN: JAZZ
At the Main menu, press Left, Up, Down, Down, Left, Up, Right.

GENERATION 1 SKIN: MEGATRON
At the Main menu, press Down, Left, Left, Down, Right, Down, Up.

GENERATION 1 SKIN: OPTIMUS PRIME
At the Main menu, press Down, Right, Left, Up, Down, Down, Left.

GENERATION 1 SKIN: ROBOVISION OPTIMUS PRIME
At the Main menu, press Down, Down, Up, Up, Right, Right, Right.

GENERATION 1 SKIN: STARSCREAM
At the Main menu, press Right, Down, Left, Left, Down, Up, Up.

TRANSFORMERS REVENGE OF THE FALLEN

LOW GRAVITY MODE
Select Cheat Code and enter ✖, ⬤, ▲, L3, ⬤, L3.

NO WEAPON OVERHEAT
Select Cheat Code and enter L3, ⬤, ✖, L3, ⬤, L1.

ALWAYS IN OVERDRIVE MODE

Select Cheat Code and enter L1, ◉, L1, ✪, ◉, R3.

UNLIMITED TURBO

Select Cheat Code and enter ◉, L3, ◉, R3, ✪, ▲

NO SPECIAL COOLDOWN TIME

Select Cheat Code and enter R3, ◉, R3, R3, ◉, ✪.

INVINCIBILITY

Select Cheat Code and enter R3, ✪, ◉, L3, ◉, ◉.

4X ENERGON FROM DEFEATED ENEMIES

Select Cheat Code and enter ▲, ◉, ◉, R3, ✪, ▲.

INCREASED WEAPON DAMAGE(ROBOT FORM)

Select the Cheat Code option and enter ▲, ▲, R3, ✪, L1, ▲.

INCREASED WEAPON DAMAGE(VEHICLE FORM)

Select Cheat Code and enter ▲, ◉, R1, ✪, R3, L3.

MELEE INSTANT KILLS

Select the Cheat Code option and enter R3, ✪. L1, ◉, R3, L1.

LOWER ENEMY ACCURACY

Select Cheat Code and enter ✪, L3, R3, L3, R3, R1.

INCREASED ENEMY HEALTH

Select Cheat Code and enter ◉, ✪, L1, ◉, R3, ▲.

INCREASED ENEMY DAMAGE

Select Cheat Code and enter L1, ▲, ✪, ▲, R3, R3.

INCREASED ENEMY ACCURACY

Select Cheat Code and enter ▲, ▲, ◉, ✪, A, L1.

SPECIAL KILLS ONLY MODE

Select Cheat Code and enter ◉, ◉, R1, ◉, ✪, L3.

UNLOCK ALL SHANGHAI MISSIONS & ZONES

Select Cheat Code and enter ▲, L3, R3, L1, ▲, ✪.

UNLOCK ALL WEST COAST MISSIONS & ZONES

Select Cheat Code and enter L1, R1, R3, ▲, R3, ◉.

UNLOCK ALL DEEP SIX MISSIONS & ZONES

Select Cheat Code and enter ✪, R1, ▲, ◉, ✪, L1.

UNLOCK ALL EAST COAST MISSIONS & ZONES

Select Cheat Code and enter R3, L3, R1, ✪, ◉, ✪.

UNLOCK ALL CAIRO MISSIONS & ZONES

Select Cheat Code and enter R3, ▲, ✪, ▲, L3, L1.

UNLOCK & ACTIVATE ALL UPGRADES

Select Cheat Code and enter L1, ▲, L1, ◉, ✪, ✪.

UNCHARTED 2: AMONG THIEVES

In Uncharted 2: Among Thieves, upon opening the store you'll have the option to hit the Square button to check for Uncharted: Drake's Fortune save data. You'll obtain cash for having save data! This cash can be used in the single and multiplayer stores. Could be useful if you want a head start online!

$20,000

Have a saved game of Uncharted: Drake's Fortune.

$80,000

Have a saved game of Uncharted: Drake's Fortune with the story completed at least once.

VIRTUA FIGHTER 5

WATCH MODE

Select Exhibition Mode, then at the character select, hold **L1** + **R1** and press ✗.

WALL-E

The following cheats will disable saving. The five possible characters starting with Wall-E and going down are: Wall-E, Auto, EVE, M-O, GEL-A Steward.

ALL BONUS FEATURES UNLOCKED

Select Cheats from the Bonus Features menu and enter Wall-E, Auto, EVE, GEL-A Steward.

ALL GAME CONTENT UNLOCKED

Select Cheats from the Bonus Features menu and enter M-O, Auto, GEL-A Steward, EVE.

ALL SINGLE-PLAYER LEVELS UNLOCKED

Select Cheats from the Bonus Features menu and enter Auto, GEL-A Steward, M-O, Wall-E.

ALL MULTIPLAYER MAPS UNLOCKED

Select Cheats from the Bonus Features menu and enter EVE, M-O, Wall-E, Auto.

ALL HOLIDAY COSTUMES UNLOCKED

Select Cheats from the Bonus Features menu and enter Auto, Auto, GEL-A Steward, GEL-A Steward.

ALL MULTIPLAYER COSTUMES UNLOCKED

Select Cheats from the Bonus Features menu and enter GEL-A Steward, Wall-E, M-O, Auto.

UNLIMITED HEALTH UNLOCKED

Select Cheats from the Bonus Features menu and enter Wall-E, M-O, Auto, M-O.

WALL-E: MAKE ANY CUBE AT ANY TIME

Select Cheats from the Bonus Features menu and enter Auto, M-O, Auto, M-O.

WALL-EVE: MAKE ANY CUBE AT ANY TIME

Select Cheats from the Bonus Features menu and enter M-O, GEL-A Steward, EVE, EVE.

WALL-E WITH A LASER GUN AT ANY TIME

Select Cheats from the Bonus Features menu and enter Wall-E, EVE, EVE, Wall-E.

WALL-EVE WITH A LASER GUN AT ANY TIME

Select Cheats from the Bonus Features menu and enter GEL-A Steward, EVE, M-O, Wall-E.

WALL-E: PERMANENT SUPER LASER UPGRADE

Select Cheats from the Bonus Features menu and enter Wall-E, Auto, EVE, M-O.

EVE: PERMANENT SUPER LASER UPGRADE

Select Cheats from the Bonus Features menu and enter EVE, Wall-E, Wall-E, Auto.

CREDITS

Select Cheats from the Bonus Features menu and enter Auto, Wall-E, GEL-A Steward, M-O.

WORLD SERIES OF POKER 2008: BATTLE FOR THE BRACELETS

PHILLIP J. HELLMUTH

Enter BEATTHEBRAT as the player name.

WWE SMACKDOWN! VS. RAW 2008

HBK AND HHH'S DX OUTFIT
Select Cheat Codes from the Options and enter DXCostume69K2.

KELLY KELLY'S ALTERNATE OUTFIT
Select Cheat Codes from the Options and enter KellyKG12R.

BRET HART
Complete the March 31, 1996 Hall of Fame challenge by defeating Bret Hart with Shawn Michaels in a One-On-One 30-Minute Iron Man Match on Legend difficulty. Purchase from WWE Shop for $210,000.

MICK FOLEY
Complete the June 28, 1998 Hall of Fame challenge by defeating Mick Foley with The Undertaker in a H*** In a Cell Match on Legend difficulty. Purchase from WWE Shop for $210,000.

MR. MCMAHON
Win or successfully defend a championship (WWE or World Heavyweight) at WrestleMania in WWE 24/7 GM Mode. Purchase from WWE Shop for $110,000.

THE ROCK
Complete the April 1, 2001 Hall of Fame challenge by defeating The Rock with Steve Austin in a Single Match on Legend Difficulty. Purchase from WWE Shop for $210,000.

STEVE AUSTIN
Complete the March 23, 1997 Hall of Fame challenge by defeating Steve Austin with Bret Hart in a Submission Match on Legend Difficulty. Purchase from WWE Shop for $210,000.

TERRY FUNK
Complete the April 13, 1997 Hall of Fame challenge by defeating Tommy Dreamer, Sabu and Sandman with any Superstar in an ECW Extreme Rules 4-Way Match on Legend difficulty. Purchase from WWE Shop for $210,000.

MR. MCMAHON BALD
Must unlock Mr. McMahon as a playable character first. Purchase from WWE Shop for $60,000.

WWE SMACKDOWN VS. RAW 2010

THE ROCK
Select Cheat Codes from the Options menu and enter The Great One.

VINCE'S OFFICE AND DIRT SHEET FOR BACKSTAGE BRAWL
Select Cheat Codes from the Options menu and enter BonusBrawl.

SHAWN MICHAELS' NEW COSTUME
Select Cheat Codes from the Options menu and enter Bow Down.

RANDY ORTON'S NEW COSTUME
Select Cheat Codes from the Options menu and enter ViperRKO.

TRIPLE H'S NEW COSTUME
Select Cheat Codes from the Options menu and enter Suck IT!.

NINTENDO Wii™

CONTENTS

NINTENDO Wii™ VIRTUAL CONSOLE GAMES

CONTENTS

ASTRO BOY: THE VIDEO GAME

INVULNERABLE

Pause the game and press Up, Down, Down, Up, 1, 2.

MAX STATS

Pause the game and press Left, Left, 2, Down, Down, 1.

INFINITE SUPERS

Pause the game and press Left, 1, Right, 1, Up, Down.

INFINITE DASHES
Pause the game and press 2, 2, 1, 2, Left, Up.

DISABLE SUPERS
Pause the game and press 1, 1, 2, 2, 1, Left.

COSTUME SWAP (ARENA AND CLASSIC COSTUMES)
Pause the game and press 2, Up, 1, Up, Down, 2.

UNLOCK LEVELS
Pause the game and press Up, 1, Right, 1, Down, 1. This allows you to travel to any level from the Story menu.

AVATAR: THE LAST AIRBENDER

UNLIMITED HEALTH
Select Code Entry from Extras and enter 94677.

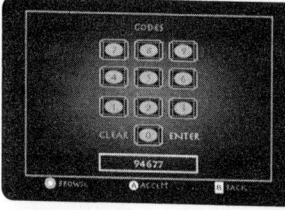 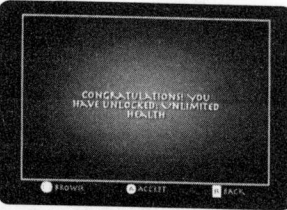

UNLIMITED CHI
Select Code Entry from Extras and enter 24463.

UNLIMITED COPPER
Select Code Entry from Extras and enter 23637.

NEVERENDING STEALTH
Select Code Entry from Extras and enter 53467.

1 HIT DISHONOR
Select Code Entry from Extras and enter 54641.

DOUBLE DAMAGE
Select Code Entry from Extras and enter 34743.

ALL TREASURE MAPS
Select Code Entry from Extras and enter 37437.

THE CHARACTER CONCEPT ART GALLERY
Select Code Entry from Extras and enter 97831.

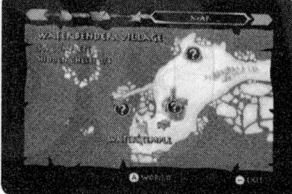 

AVATAR: THE LAST AIRBENDER-THE BURNING EARTH

DOUBLE DAMAGE
Go to the code entry section and enter 90210.

INFINITE LIFE
Go to the code entry section and enter 65049.

INFINITE SPECIAL ATTACKS
Go to the code entry section and enter 66206.

MAX LEVEL
Go to the code entry section and enter 89121.

ONE-HIT DISHONOR
Go to the code entry section and enter 28260.

ALL BONUS GAMES
Go to the code entry section and enter 99801.

ALL GALLERY ITEMS
Go to the code entry section and enter 85061.

AVATAR - THE LAST AIRBENDER: INTO THE INFERNO

After you have defeated the first level, The Awakening, go to Ember Island. Walk to the left past the volleyball net to a red and yellow door. Select Game Secrets and then Code Entry. Now you can enter the following cheats.

MAX COINS
Enter 66639224.

ALL ITEMS AVAILABLE FROM SHOP
Enter 34737253.

ALL CHAPTERS
Enter 52993833.

UNLOCK CONCEPT ART IN GALLERY
Enter 27858343.

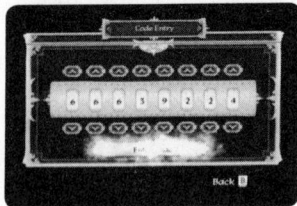

BEN 10: PROTECTOR OF EARTH

INVINCIBILITY
Select a game from the Continue option. Go to the Map Selection screen, press Plus and choose Extras. Select Enter Secret Code and enter XLR8, Heatblast, Wildvine, Fourarms.

ALL COMBOS
Select a game from the Continue option. Go to the Map Selection screen, press Plus and choose Extras. Select Enter Secret Code and enter Cannonblot, Heatblast, Fourarms, Heatblast.

ALL LOCATIONS

Select a game from the Continue option. Go to the Map Selection screen, press Plus and choose Extras. Select Enter Secret Code and enter Heatblast, XLR8, XLR8, Cannonblot.

DNA FORCE SKINS

Select a game from the Continue option. Go to the Map Selection screen, press Plus and choose Extras. Select Enter Secret Code and enter Wildvine, Fourarms, Heatblast, Cannonbolt.

DARK HEROES SKINS

Select a game from the Continue option. Go to the Map Selection screen, press Plus and choose Extras. Select Enter Secret Code and enter Cannonbolt, Cannonbolt, Fourarms, Heatblast.

ALL ALIEN FORMS

Select a game from the Continue option. Go to the Map Selection screen, press Plus and choose Extras. Select Enter Secret Code and enter Wildvine, Fourarms, Heatblast, Wildvine.

MASTER CONTROL

Select a game from the Continue option. Go to the Map Selection screen, press Plus and choose Extras. Select Enter Secret Code and enter Cannonbolt, Heatblast, Wildvine, Fourarms.

BLAZING ANGELS: SQUADRONS OF WWII

ALL AIRCRAFT AND CAMPAIGNS

After you have chosen a pilot, hold Minus + Plus and press Left, Right, 1, 2, 2, 1.

GOD MODE

Pause the game, hold Minus and press 1, 2, 1, 2.

WEAPON DAMAGE INCREASED

Pause the game, hold Minus and press 2, 1, 1, 2.

BOOM BLOX

ALL TOYS IN CREATE MODE

At the title screen, press Up, Right, Down, Left to bring up a cheats menu. Enter Tool Pool.

SLOW-MO IN SINGLE PLAYER

At the title screen, press Up, Right, Down, Left to bring up a cheats menu. Enter Blox Time.

CHEERLEADERS BECOME PROFILE CHARACTER

At the title screen, press Up, Right, Down, Left to bring up a cheats menu. Enter My Team.

FLOWER EXPLOSIONS

At the title screen, press Up, Right, Down, Left to bring up a cheats menu. Enter Flower Power.

JINGLE BLOCKS

At the title screen, press Up, Right, Down, Left to bring up a cheats menu. Enter Maestro.

BUILD-A-BEAR WORKSHOP: A FRIEND FUR ALL SEASONS

ALL ISLANDS, MINIGAMES, OUTFITS, AND ACCESSORIES

At the main menu, press Up, Down, Left, Right, A, B.

CARS MATER-NATIONAL

ALL ARCADE RACES, MINI-GAMES, AND WORLDS

Select Codes/Cheats from the options and enter PLAYALL.

ALL CARS

Select Codes/Cheats from the options and enter MATTEL07.

ALTERNATE LIGHTNING MCQUEEN COLORS

Select Codes/Cheats from the options and enter NCEDUDZ.

ALL COLORS FOR OTHERS

Select Codes/Cheats from the options and enter PAINTIT.

UNLIMITED TURBO

Select Codes/Cheats from the options and enter ZZOOOOM.

EXTREME ACCELERATION

Select Codes/Cheats from the options and enter 0TO200X.

EXPERT MODE

Select Codes/Cheats from the options and enter VRYFAST.

ALL BONUS ART

Select Codes/Cheats from the options and enter BUYTALL.

CARS RACE-O-RAMA

ALL ARCADE MODE EVENTS

Select Cheats from the Options menu and enter SLVRKEY.

 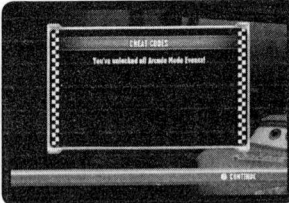

ALL STORY MODE EVENTS

Select Cheats from the Options menu and enter GOLDKEY.

ALL OF LIGHTNING MCQUEEN'S FRIENDS

Select Cheats from the Options menu and enter EVRYBDY.

ALL LIGHTNING MCQUEEN CUSTOM KIT PARTS

Select Cheats from the Options menu and enter GR8MODS.

ALL PAINT JOBS FOR ALL NON-LIGHTNING MCQUEEN CHARACTERS

Select Cheats from the Options menu and enter CARSHOW.

CODE LYOKO: QUEST FOR INFINITY

UNLOCK EVERYTHING
Pause the game and press 2, 1, C, Z, 2, 1.

UNLIMITED HEALTH AND POWER
Pause the game and press 2, 2, Z, Z, 1, 1.

INCREASE SPEED
Pause the game and press Z, 1, 2, 1 (x3).

INCREASE DAMAGE
Pause the game and press 1, Z, Z, C (x3).

CONFIGURATION A
Pause the game and press 2, Z, 1, Z, C, Z.

CONFIGURATION B
Pause the game and press C, C, 1, C, Z, C.

ALL ABILITIES
Pause the game and press Z, C, Z, C (x3).

ALL BONUSES
Pause the game and press 1, 2, C, 2 (x3).

ALL GOODIES
Pause the game and press C, 2, 2, Z, C, Z.

CONTRA REBIRTH

DEBUG MENU
At the title screen, press Plus + 1 + 2.

CORALINE

UNLIMITED LEVEL SKIP
Select Cheats from the Options menu and enter Beldam.

UNLIMITED HEALTH
Select Cheats from the Options menu and enter beets.

UNLIMITED FIREFLYS
Select Cheats from the Options menu and enter garden.

FREE HALL PASSES
Select Cheats from the Options menu and enter well.

BUTTON EYE CORALINE
Select Cheats from the Options menu and enter cheese.

DE BLOB

INVULNERABILITY
During a game, hold C and press 1, 1, 1, 1.
Re-enter the code to disable.

LIFE UP
During a game, hold C and press 1, 1, 2, 2

TIME BONUS
During a game, hold C and press 1, 2, 1, 2.
This adds 10 minutes to your time.

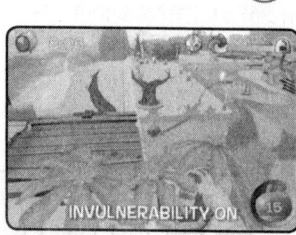

ALL MOODS
At the main menu, hold C and press B, B, 1, 2, 1, 2, B, B.

ALL MULTIPLAYER LEVELS

At the main menu, hold C and press 2, 2, B, B, 1, 1, B, B.

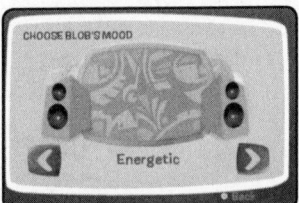
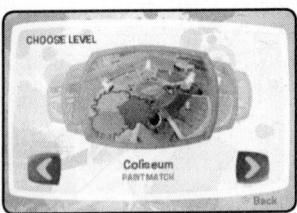

DEFEND YOUR CASTLE

GIANT ENEMIES

Select Credits and click SMB3W4 when it appears.

TINY UNITS

Select Credits and click Chuck Norris when it appears.

EASY LEVEL COMPLETE

Pause the game and wait for the sun to set. Unpause to complete the level.

DISNEY PRINCESS: ENCHANTED JOURNEY

BELLE'S KINGDOM

Select Secrets and enter GASTON.

GOLDEN SET

Select Secrets and enter BLUEBIRD.

FLOWER WAND

Select Secrets and enter SLEEPY.

HEART WAND

Select Secrets and enter BASHFUL.

SHELL WAND

Select Secrets and enter RAJAH.

SHIELD WAND

Select Secrets and enter CHIP.

STAR WAND

Select Secrets and enter SNEEZY.

DONKEY KONG COUNTRY 2: DIDDY'S KONG QUEST

SOUND TEST

Highlight Two Player and press Down (x5).

CHEAT MODE

Press Down (x5) again after getting Sound Test to access the cheat mode. Now you can enter the following:

50 LIVES

Press Y, A, Select, A, Down, Left, A, Down.

HARD MODE

Press B, A, Right, Right, A, Left, A, X. This gets rid of the barrels.

DRAGON BALL Z: BUDOKAI TENKAICHI 2

Hold Z + Minus to clear codes.

DOUBLE FIST POWER

At the Stage Select in vs mode, hold Z + Plus to start code input. Swing the Nunchuk Right, Wiimote Left, Wiimote Left + Nunchuk Right, Wiimote and Nunchuk Down.

TAIL POWER

At the Stage Select in vs mode, hold Z + Plus to start code input. Swing the Wiimote Down, Up, Left, Right.

DRAGON BALL Z: BUDOKAI TENKAICHI 3

SURVIVAL MODE

Clear 30 missions in Mission 100 mode.

DRAGON BLADE: WRATH OF FIRE

ALL LEVELS

At the title screen, hold Plus + Minus and select New Game or Load game. Hold the buttons until the stage select appears.

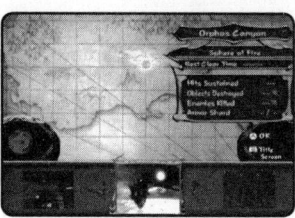

EASY DIFFICULTY

At the title screen, hold Z + 2 when selecting "New Game."

HARD DIFFICLUTY

At the title screen, hold C + 2 when selecting "New Game."
To clear the following codes, hold Z at the stage select.

DRAGON HEAD

At the stage select, hold Z and press Plus. Immediately Swing Wii Remote Right, swing Wii Remote Down, swing Nunchuk Left, swing Nunchuk Right.

DRAGON WINGS

At the stage select, hold Z and press Plus. Immediately Swing Nunchuk Up + Wii Remote Up, swing Nunchuk Down + Wii Remote Down, swing Nunchuk Right + Wii Remote Left, swing Nunchuk Left + Wii Remote Right.

TAIL POWER

At the stage select, hold Z and press Plus. Immediately Swing your Wii Remote Down, Up, Left, and Right.

DOUBLE FIST POWER

At the stage select, hold Z and press Plus. Immediately swing your Nunchuk Right; swing your Wii Remote left; swing your Nunchuk right while swinging your Wii Remote left; swing both the Wii Remote and the Nunchuk down.

FAMILY FEUD 2010 EDITION

NEW WARDROBE

Select the lock tab from the Wardrobe screen and enter FAMILY.

GHOST SQUAD

COSTUMES

Reach the following levels in single-player to unlock the corresponding costume.

LEVEL	COSTUME	LEVEL	COSTUME
07	Desert Camouflage	30	Urban Camouflage
10	Policeman	34	Virtua Cop
15	Tough Guy	38	Future Warrior
18	Sky Camouflage	50	Ninja
20	World War II	60	Panda Suit
23	Cowboy	99	Gold Uniform

NINJA MODE

Play through Arcade Mode.

PARADISE MODE

Play through Ninja Mode.

G.I. JOE: THE RISE OF COBRA

CLASSIC DUKE

At the title screen press Left, Up, -, Up, Right, +.

CLASSIC SCARLETT

At the title screen press Right, Up, Down, Down, +.

GODZILLA UNLEASHED

UNLOCK ALL

At the main menu, press A + Up to bring up the cheat entry screen. Enter 204935.

90000 STORE POINTS

At the main menu, press A + Up to bring up the cheat entry screen. Enter 031406.

SET DAY

At the main menu, press A + Up to bring up the cheat entry screen. Enter 0829XX, where XX represents the day. Use 00 for day one.

SHOW MONSTER MOVES

At the main menu, press A + Up to bring up the cheat entry screen. Enter 411411.

VERSION NUMBER

At the main menu, press A + Up to bring up the cheat entry screen. Enter 787321.

MOTHERSHIP LEVEL

Playing as the Aliens, destroy the mothership in the Invasion level.

GRADIUS REBIRTH

4 OPTIONS

Pause the game and press Up, Up, Down, Down, Left, Right, Left, Right, Fire, Powerup. This code can be used once for each stage you have attempted.

GRAVITRONIX

VERSUS OPTIONS AND LEVEL SELECT
At the Options menu, press 1, 2, 2, 2, 1.

THE GRIM ADVENTURES OF BILLY & MANDY

CONCEPT ART
At the Main menu, hold 1 and press Up, Up, Down, Down, Left, Right, Left, Right.

ICE AGE 2: THE MELTDOWN

INFINITE PEBBLES
Pause the game and press Down, Down, Left, Up, Up, Right, Up, Down.

INFINITE ENERGY
Pause the game and press Down, Left, Right, Down, Down, Right, Left, Down.

INFINITE HEALTH
Pause the game and press Up, Right, Down, Up, Left, Down, Right, Left.

INDIANA JONES AND THE STAFF OF KINGS

FATE OF ATLANTIS GAME
At the main menu, hold Z and press A, Up, Up, B, Down, Down, Left, Right, Left, B.

IRON MAN

ARMOR SELECTION
Iron Man's different armor suits are unlocked by completing certain missions. Refer to the following tables for when each is unlocked. After selecting a mission to play, you get the opportunity to pick the armor you wish to use.

COMPLETE MISSION	SUIT UNLOCKED
1: Escape	Mark I
2: First Flight	Mark II
3: Fight Back	Mark III
6: Flying Fortress	Comic Tin Can
9: Home Front	Classic
13: Showdown	Silver Centurion

CONCEPT ART
Concept Art is unlocked after finding certain numbers of Weapon Crates.

CONCEPT ART UNLOCKED	NUMBER OF WEAPON CRATES FOUND
Environments Set 1	6
Environments Set 2	12
Iron Man	18
Environments Set 3	24
Enemies	30
Environments Set 4	36
Villains	42
Vehicles	48
Covers	50

KUNG FU PANDA

INFINITE CHI
Select Cheats from the Extra menu and press Down, Right, Left, Up, Down.

INVINCIBILITY
Select Cheats from the Extra menu and press Down, Down, Right, Up, Left.

4X DAMAGE MULTIPLYER
Select Cheats from the Extra menu and press Up, Down, Up, Right, Left.

ALL MULTIPLAYER CHARACTERS
Select Cheats from the Extra menu and press Left, Down, Left, Right, Down.

DRAGON WARRIOR OUTFIT IN MULTIPLAYER
Select Cheats from the Extra menu and press Left, Down, Right, Left, Up.

THE LEGEND OF SPYRO: DAWN OF THE DRAGON

INFINITE HEALTH
Pause the game, hold Z and move the Nunchuk Right, Right, Down, Down, Left.

INFINITE MANA
Pause the game, hold Z and move the Nunchuk Up, Right, Up, Left, Down.

MAX XP
Pause the game, hold Z and move the Nunchuk Up, Left, Left, Down, Up.

ALL ELEMENTAL UPGRADES
Pause the game, hold Z and move the Nunchuk Left, Up, Down, Up, Right.

LEGO BATMAN

BATCAVE CODES
Using the computer in the Batcave, select Enter Code and enter the following codes.

CHARACTERS

CHARACTER	CODE	CHARACTER	CODE
Alfred	ZAQ637	Penguin Henchman	BJH782
Batgirl	JKR331	Penguin Minion	KJP748
Bruce Wayne	BDJ327	Poison Ivy Goon	GTB899
Catwoman (Classic)	M1AAWW	Police Marksman	HKG984
Clown Goon	HJK327	Police Officer	JRY983
Commissioner Gordon	DDP967	Riddler Goon	CRY928
Fishmonger	HGY748	Riddler Henchman	XEU824
Freeze Girl	XVK541	S.W.A.T.	HTF114
Joker Goon	UTF782	Sailor	NAV592
Joker Henchman	YUN924	Scientist	JFL786
Mad Hatter	JCA283	Security Guard	PLB946
Man-Bat	NYU942	The Joker (Tropical)	CCB199
Military Policeman	MKL382	Yeti	NJL412
Nightwing	MVY759	Zoo Sweeper	DWR243
Penguin Goon	NKA238		

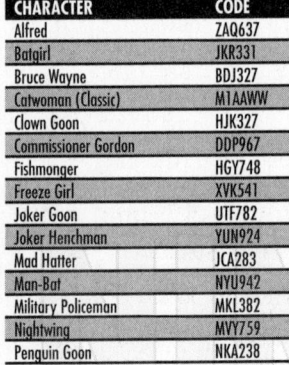

VEHICLES

VEHICLE	CODE	VEHICLE	CODE
Bat-Tank	KNTT4B	Mr. Freeze's Kart	BCT229
Bruce Wayne's Private Jet	LEA664	Penguin Goon Submarine	BTN248
Catwoman's Motorcycle	HPL826	Police Bike	LJP234
Garbage Truck	DUS483	Police Boat	PLC999
Goon Helicopter	GCH328	Police Car	KJL832
Harbor Helicopter	CHP735	Police Helicopter	CWR732
Harley Quinn's Hammer Truck	RDT637	Police Van	MAC788
Mad Hatter's Glider	HS000W	Police Watercraft	VJD328
Mad Hatter's Steamboat	M4DM4N	Riddler's Jet	HAHAHA
Mr. Freeze's Iceberg	ICYICE	Robin's Submarine	TTF453
The Joker's Van	JUK657	Two-Face's Armored Truck	EFE933

CHEATS

CHEAT	CODE	CHEAT	CODE
Always Score Multiply	9LRGNB	More Batarang Targets	XWP645
Fast Batarangs	JRBDCB	Piece Detector	KHJ554
Fast Walk	ZOLM6N	Power Brick Detector	MMN786
Flame Batarang	D8NYWH	Regenerate Hearts	HJH7HJ
Freeze Batarang	XPN4NG	Score x2	N4NR3E
Extra Hearts	ML3KHP	Score x4	CX9MAT
Fast Build	EVG26J	Score x6	MLVNF2
Immune to Freeze	JXUDY6	Score x8	WCCDB9
Invincibility	WYD5CP	Score x10	18HW07
Minikit Detector	ZXGH9J		

LEGO INDIANA JONES: THE ORIGINAL ADVENTURES

CHARACTERS

Approach the blackboard in the Classsroom and enter the following codes.

CHARACTER	CODE	CHARACTER	CODE
Bandit	12N68W	Enemy Boxer	8246RB
Bandit Swordsman	1MK4RT	Enemy Butler	VJ48W3
Barranca	04EM94	Enemy Guard	VJ7R51
Bazooka Trooper (Crusade)	MK83R7	Enemy Guard (Mountains)	YR47WM
Bazooka Trooper (Raiders)	S93Y5R	Enemy Officer	572E61
Belloq	CHN3YU	Enemy Officer (Desert)	2MK450
Belloq (Jungle)	TDR197	Enemy Pilot	B84ELP
Belloq (Robes)	VEO29L	Enemy Radio Operator	1MF94R
British Commander	B73EUA	Enemy Soldier (Desert)	4NSU7Q
British Officer	VJ5TI9	Fedora	V75YSP
British Soldier	DJ5I2W	First Mate	0GIN24
Captain Katanga	VJ3TT3	Grail Knight	NE6THI
Chatter Lal	ENW936	Hovitos Tribesman	HOV1SS
Chatter Lal (Thuggee)	CNH4RY	Indiana Jones (Desert Disguise)	4J8S4M
Chen	3NK48T	Indiana Jones (Officer)	VJ850S
Colonel Dietrich	2K9RKS	Jungle Guide	24PF34
Colonel Vogel	8EAL4H	Kao Kan	WMO46L
Dancing Girl	C7EJ21	Kazim	NRH23J
Donovan	3NFTU8	Kazim (Desert)	3M29TJ
Elsa (Desert)	JSNRT9	Lao Che	2NK479
Elsa (Officer)	VMJ5US	Maharajah	NFK5N2

57

CHARACTER	CODE
Major Toht	13NS01
Masked Bandit	N48SF0
Mola Ram	FJUR31
Monkey Man	3RF6YJ
Pankot Assassin	2NKT72
Pankot Guard	VN28RH
Sherpa Brawler	VJ37WJ
Sherpa Gunner	ND762W
Slave Child	0E3ENW

CHARACTER	CODE
Thuggee	VM683E
Thuggee Acolyte	T2R3F9
Thuggee Slave Driver	VBS7GW
Village Dignitary	KD48TN
Village Elder	4682E1
Willie (Dinner Suit)	VK93R7
Willie (Pajamas)	MEN4IP
Wu Han	3NSLT8

EXTRAS

Approach the blackboard in the Classsroom and enter the following codes. Some cheats need to be enabled by selecting Extras from the pause menu.

CHEAT	CODE
Artifact Detector	VIKED7
Beep Beep	VNF59Q
Character Treasure	VIES2R
Disarm Enemies	VKRNS9
Disguises	41D1N6
Fast Build	V83SL0
Fast Dig	378RS6
Fast Fix	FJ59WS
Fertilizer	B1GW1F
Ice Rink	33GM7J
Parcel Detector	VUT673
Poo Treasure	WWQ1SA

CHEAT	CODE
Regenerate Hearts	MDLP69
Secret Characters	3X44AA
Silhouettes	3HE85H
Super Scream	VN3R7S
Super Slap	0P1TA5
Treasure Magnet	H86LA2
Treasure x10	VI3PS8
Treasure x2	VM4TS9
Treasure x4	VLWEN3
Treasure x6	V84RYS
Treasure x8	A72E1M

LEGO STAR WARS: THE COMPLETE SAGA

The following still need to be purchase after entering the codes.

CHARACTERS

ADMIRAL ACKBAR

At the bar in Mos Eisley Cantina, select Enter Code and enter ACK646.

BATTLE DROID (COMMANDER)

At the bar in Mos Eisley Cantina, select Enter Code and enter KPF958.

BOBA FETT (BOY)

At the bar in Mos Eisley Cantina, select Enter Code and enter GGF539.

BOSS NASS

At the bar in Mos Eisley Cantina, select Enter Code and enter HHY697.

CAPTAIN TARPALS

At the bar in Mos Eisley Cantina, select Enter Code and enter QRN714.

COUNT DOOKU

At the bar in Mos Eisley Cantina, select Enter Code and enter DDD748.

DARTH MAUL

At the bar in Mos Eisley Cantina, select Enter Code and enter EUK421.

EWOK

At the bar in Mos Eisley Cantina, select Enter Code and enter EWK785.

GENERAL GRIEVOUS

At the bar in Mos Eisley Cantina, select Enter Code and enter PMN576.

GREEDO

At the bar in Mos Eisley Cantina, select Enter Code and enter ZZR636.

IG-88

At the bar in Mos Eisley Cantina, select Enter Code and enter GIJ989.

IMPERIAL GUARD

At the bar in Mos Eisley Cantina, select Enter Code and enter GUA850.

JANGO FETT

At the bar in Mos Eisley Cantina, select Enter Code and enter KLJ897.

KI-ADI MUNDI

At the bar in Mos Eisley Cantina, select Enter Code and enter MUN486.

LUMINARA

At the bar in Mos Eisley Cantina, select Enter Code and enter LUM521.

PADMÉ

At the bar in Mos Eisley Cantina, select Enter Code and enter VBJ322.

R2-Q5

At the bar in Mos Eisley Cantina, select Enter Code and enter EVILR2.

STORMTROOPER

At the bar in Mos Eisley Cantina, select Enter Code and enter NBN431.

TAUN WE

At the bar in Mos Eisley Cantina, select Enter Code and enter PRX482.

VULTURE DROID

At the bar in Mos Eisley Cantina, select Enter Code and enter BDC866.

WATTO

At the bar in Mos Eisley Cantina, select Enter Code and enter PLL967.

ZAM WESELL

At the bar in Mos Eisley Cantina, select Enter Code and enter 584HJF.

SKILLS

DISGUISE

At the bar in Mos Eisley Cantina, select Enter Code and enter BRJ437.

FORCE GRAPPLE LEAP

At the bar in Mos Eisley Cantina, select Enter Code and enter CLZ738.

VEHICLES

DROID TRIFIGHTER

At the bar in Mos Eisley Cantina, select Enter Code and enter AAB123.

IMPERIAL SHUTTLE

At the bar in Mos Eisley Cantina, select Enter Code and enter HUT845.

TIE INTERCEPTOR

At the bar in Mos Eisley Cantina, select Enter Code and enter INT729.

TIE FIGHTER

At the bar in Mos Eisley Cantina, select Enter Code and enter DBH897.

ZAM'S AIRSPEEDER

At the bar in Mos Eisley Cantina, select Enter
Code and enter UUU875.

MADDEN NFL 10

UNLOCK EVERYTHING

Select Enter Game Code from Extras and enter THEWORKS.

FRANCHISE MODE

Select Enter Game Code from Extras and enter TEAMPLAYER.

SITUATION MODE

Select Enter Game Code from Extras and enter YOUCALLIT.

SUPERSTAR MODE

Select Enter Game Code from Extras and enter EGOBOOST.

PRO BOWL STADIUM

Select Enter Game Code from Extras and enter ALLSTARS.

SUPER BOWL STADIUM

Select Enter Game Code from Extras and enter THEBIGSHOW.

MADSTONE

HIGH GRAVITY

At the main menu press Down, Down, Down, Down, Right, Left, Right, Left.

LOW GRAVITY

At the main menu press Up, Up, Left, Left, Up, Up, Right, Right.

PLAYER SKULLS IN ARCADE MODE

At the difficulty select press Up, Right, Down, Left, Up, Right, Down, Left.

SAVANT MODE IN ARCADE MODE

At the difficulty select, press Down (x10).

MARBLE SAGA: KORORINPA

MASTER HIGGINS BALL
Select ??? from the Options. Press A on the right lamp, the left lamp twice, and the right lamp again. Now select the right icon and enter TV, Car, Sunflower, Bike, Helicopter, Strawberry.

MIRROR MODE
Select ??? from the Options. Press A on the right lamp, the left lamp twice, and the right lamp again. Now select the right icon and enter Beetle, Clover, Boy, Plane, Car, Bike.

MARIO & SONIC AT THE OLYMPIC GAMES

UNLOCK 4X100M RELAY EVENT
Medal in Mercury, Venus, Jupiter, and Saturn.

UNLOCK SINGLE SCULLS EVENT
Medal in Mercury, Venus, Jupiter, and Saturn.

UNLOCK DREAM RACE EVENT
Medal in Mercury, Venus, Jupiter, and Saturn.

UNLOCK ARCHERY EVENT
Medal in Moonlight Circuit.

UNLOCK HIGH JUMP EVENT
Medal in Stardust Circuit.

UNLOCK 400M EVENT
Medal in Planet Circuit.

UNLOCK DREAM FENCING EVENT
Medal in Comet Circuit.

UNLOCK DREAM TABLE TENNIS EVENT
Medal in Satellite Circuit.

UNLOCK 400M HURDLES EVENT
Medal in Sunlight Circuit.

UNLOCK POLE VAULT EVENT
Medal in Meteorite Circuit.

UNLOCK VAULT EVENT
Medal in Meteorite Circuit.

UNLOCK DREAM PLATFORM EVENT
Medal in Cosmos Circuit.

CROWNS
Get all gold medals in all events with a character to unlock their crown.

MARIO KART WII

CHARACTERS

CHARACTER	HOW TO UNLOCK
Baby Daisy	Earn 1 Star in 50cc for Mushroom, Flower, Star, and Special Cups
Baby Luigi	Unlock 8 Expert Staff Ghost Data in Time Trials
Birdo	Race 16 different courses in Time Trials or win 250 versus races
Bowser Jr.	Earn 1 Star in 100cc for Shell, Banana, Leaf, and Lightning Cups
Daisy	Win 150cc Special Cup
Diddy Kong	Win 50cc Lightning Cup
Dry Bones	Win 100cc Leaf Cup
Dry Bowser	Earn 1 Star in 150cc for Mushroom, Flower, Star, and Special Cups
Funky Kong	Unlock 4 Expert Staff Ghost Data in Time Trials
King Boo	Win 50cc Star Cup
Mii Outfit A	Win 100cc Special Cup
Mii Outfit B	Unlock all 32 Expert Staff Ghost Data in Time Trials
Mii Outfit C	Get 15,000 points in Versus Mode
Rosalina	Have a Super Mario Galaxy save file and she is unlocked after 50 races or earn 1 Star in all Mirror Cups
Toadette	Race 32 different courses in Time Trials

KARTS

KART	HOW TO UNLOCK
Blue Falcon	Win Mirror Lightning Cup
Cheep Charger	Earn 1 Star in 50cc for Mushroom, Flower, Star, and Special Cups
Rally Romper	Unlock an Expert Staff Ghost Data in Time Trials
B Dasher Mk. 2	Unlock 24 Expert Staff Ghost Data in Time Trials
Royal Racer	Win 150cc Leaf Cup
Turbo Blooper	Win 50cc Leaf Cup
Aero Glider	Earn 1 Star in 150cc for Mushroom, Flower, Star, and Special Cups
Dragonetti	Win 150cc Lightning Cup
Piranha Prowler	Win 50cc Special Cup

BIKES

KART	HOW TO UNLOCK
Bubble Bike	Win Mirror Leaf Cup
Magikruiser	Race 8 different courses in Time Trials
Quacker	Win 150cc Star Cup
Dolphin Dasher	Win Mirror Star Cup
Nitrocycle	Earn 1 Star in 100cc for all cups
Rapide	Win 100cc Lightning Cup
Phantom	Win Mirror Special Cup
Torpedo	Unlock 12 Expert Staff Ghost Data in Time Trials
Twinkle Star	Win 100cc Star Cup

MARVEL SUPER HERO SQUAD

IRON MAN BONUS COSTUMES

Select Enter Code from the Options and enter 111111.

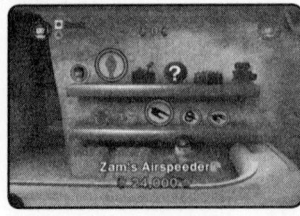 

HULK BONUS COSTUMES

Select Enter Code from the Options and enter 222222.

WOLVERINE BONUS COSTUMES

Select Enter Code from the Options and enter 333333.

THOR BONUS COSTUMES

Select Enter Code from the Options and enter 444444.

SILVER SURFER BONUS COSTUMES

Select Enter Code from the Options and enter 555555.

FALCON BONUS COSTUMES

Select Enter Code from the Options and enter 666666.

CHEAT SUPER KNOCKBACK

Select Enter Code from the Options and enter 777777.

CHEAT NO BLOCK MODE
Select Enter Code from the Options and enter 888888.
DR. DOOM BONUS COSTUMES
Select Enter Code from the Options and enter 999999.

MARVEL ULTIMATE ALLIANCE

UNLOCK ALL SKINS
At the Team menu, press Up, Down, Left, Right, Left, Right, Plus.

UNLOCKS ALL HERO POWERS
At the Team menu, press Left, Right, Up, Down, Up, Down, Plus.

ALL HEROES TO LEVEL 99
At the Team menu, press Up, Left, Up, Left, Down, Right, Down, Right, Plus.

UNLOCK ALL HEROES
At the Team menu, press Up, Up, Down, Down, Left, Left, Left, Plus.

UNLOCK DAREDEVIL
At the Team menu, press Left, Left, Right, Right, Up, Down, Up, Down, Plus.

UNLOCK SILVER SURFER
At the Team menu, press Down, Left, Left, Up, Right, Up, Down, Left, Plus.

GOD MODE
During gameplay, press Up, Down, Up, Down, Up, Left, Down, Right, Plus.

TOUCH OF DEATH
During gameplay, press Left, Right, Down, Down, Right, Left, Plus.

SUPER SPEED
During gameplay, press Up, Left, Up, Right, Down, Right, Plus.

FILL MOMENTUM
During gameplay, press Left, Right, Right, Left, Up, Down, Down, Up, Plus.

UNLOCK ALL COMICS
At the Review menu, press Left, Right, Right, Left, Up, Up, Right, Plus.

UNLOCK ALL CONCEPT ART
At the Review menu, press Down, Down, Down, Right, Right, Left, Down, Plus.

UNLOCK ALL CINEMATICS
At the Review menu, press Up, Left, Left, Up, Right, Right, Up, Plus.

UNLOCK ALL LOAD SCREENS
At the Review menu, press Up, Down, Right, Left, Up, Up Down, Plus.

UNLOCK ALL COURSES
At the Comic Missions menu, press Up, Right, Left, Down, Up, Right, Left, Down, Plus.

MARVEL: ULTIMATE ALLIANCE 2

GOD MODE
At any point during a game, press Up, Up, Down, Down, Left, Right, Down.

GIVE MONEY
At the Team Select or Hero Details screen press Up, Up, Down, Down, Up, Up, Up, Down.

UNLOCK ALL POWERS
At the Team Select or Hero Details screen press Up, Up, Down, Down, Left, Right, Right, Left.

ADVANCE ALL CHARACTERS TO L99
At the Hero Details screen press Down, Up, Left, Up, Right, Up, Left, Down.

UNLOCK ALL BONUS MISSIONS
While using the Bonus Mission Simulator, press Up, Right, Down, Left, Left, Right, Up, Up.

ADD 1 CHARACTER LEVEL

During a game, press Down, Up, Right, Up, Right, Up, Right, Down.

ADD 10 CHARACTER LEVELS

During a game, press Down, Up, Left, Up, Left, Up, Left, Down.

MLB POWER PROS

EXTRA FORMS

At the main menu, press Right, Left, Up, Down, Down, Right, Right, Up, Up, Left, Down, Left.

VIEW MLB PLAYERS AT CUSTOM PLAYER MENU

Select View or Delete Custom Players/Password Display from My Data and press Up, Up, Down, Down, Left, Right, Left, Right, 1, 2.

MONSTER JAM

TRUCKS

As you collect monster points, they are tallied toward your Championship Score. Trucks are unlocked when you reach certain point totals.

TRUCK	POINTS
Destroyer	10,000
Blacksmith	50,000
El Toro Loco	70,000
Suzuki	110,000
Maximum Destruction	235,000

MYSIMS

PASSWORD SCREEN

Press the Minus button to bring up the pause screen. Then enter the following with the Wii Remote: 2, 1, Down, Up, Down, Up, Left, Left, Right, Right. Now you can enter the following passwords:

OUTFITS

Camouflage pants	N10ng5g
Diamond vest	TglgOca
Genie outfit	Gvsb3k1
Kimono dress	I3hkdvs
White jacket	R705aan

FURNITURE

Bunk bed	F3nevrO
Hourglass couch	Ghtymba
Modern couch	T7srhca
Racecar bed	Ahvmrva
Rickshaw bed	Itha7da

MYSIMS KINGDOM

DETECTIVE OUTFIT

Pause the game and press Left, Right, Left, Right, Left, Right.

SWORDSMAN OUTFIT

Pause the game and press Down, Up, Down, Up, Down, Up, Down, Up.

TATTOO VEST OUTFIT

Pause the game and press C, Z, C, Z, B, A, B, A.

MYSIMS AGENTS

ASTRONAUT SUIT

At the Create-a-Sim screen, press Up, Down, Up, Down, Left, Right, Left, Right.

BLACK NINJA OUTFIT

At the Create-a-Sim screen, press Right, Up, Right, Up, Down, Left, Down, Left.

STEALTH SUIT

At the Create-a-Sim screen, press Left, Right, Left, Right, Up, Down, Up, Down.

NASCAR KART RACING

JOEY LOGANO

Select Enter Cheat from the Profile Info menu and enter 426378.

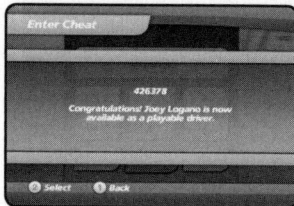 

NBA LIVE 08

AGENT ZERO SHOES

At the extras menu, enter ADGILLIT6BE as a code.

CUBA SHOES

At the extras menu, enter ADGILLIT4BC as a code.

CUSTOMIZE SHOES

At the extras menu, enter ADGILLIT5BD as a code.

DUNCAN ALL STAR SHOES

At the extras menu, enter FE454DFJCC as a code.

GIL WOOD SHOES

At the extras menu, enter ADGILLIT1B9 as a code.

GIL ZERO ALL STAR SHOES

At the extras menu, enter 23DN1PPOG4 as a code.

TS LIGHTSWITCH AWAY SHOES

At the extras menu, enter ADGILLIT0B8 as a code.

TS LIGHTSWITCH HOME SHOES

At the extras menu, enter ADGILLIT2BA as a code.

NEED FOR SPEED PROSTREET

$2,000

Select Career and then choose Code Entry. Enter 1MA9X99.

$4,000

Select Career and then choose Code Entry. Enter W2IOLL01.

$8,000

Select Career and then choose Code Entry. Enter L1IS97A1.

$10,000

Select Career and then choose Code Entry. Enter 1MI9K7E1.

$10,000

Select Career and then choose Code Entry. Enter CASHMONEY.

$10,000

Select Career and then choose Code Entry. Enter REGGAME.

AUDI TT

Select Career and then choose Code Entry. Enter ITSABOUTYOU.

CHEVELLE SS

Select Career and then choose Code Entry. Enter HORSEPOWER.

COKE ZERO GOLF GTI

Select Career and then choose Code Entry. Enter COKEZERO.

DODGE VIPER

Select Career and then choose Code Entry. Enter WORLDSLONGESTLASTING.

MITSUBISHI LANCER EVOLUTION

Select Career and then choose Code Entry. Enter MITSUBISHIGOFAR.

UNLOCK ALL BONUSES

Select Career and then choose Code Entry. Enter UNLOCKALLTHINGS.

5 REPAIR MARKERS

Select Career and then choose Code Entry. Enter SAFETYNET.

ENERGIZER VINYL

Select Career and then choose Code Entry. Enter ENERGIZERLITHIUM.

CASTROL SYNTEC VINYL

Select Career and then choose Code Entry. Enter CASTROLSYNTEC. This also gives you $10,000.

NERF N-STRIKE

BLACK HEART VENGEANCE

Select Codes from the main menu and enter BHDETA8.

CRUSHER SAD-G

Select Codes from the main menu and enter CRUSH14.

FIREFLY ELITE

Select Codes from the main menu and enter HELIOX6.

GOLIATHAN NITRO

Select Codes from the main menu and enter FIERO2.

HABANERO

Select Codes from the main menu and enter 24KGCON4.

HYDRA

Select Codes from the main menu and enter HRANGEL3.

LONGSHOT STREET

Select Codes from the main menu and enter LONGST5.

MAVERICK CRYSTAL

Select Codes from the main menu and enter CRISTOL10.

MAVERICK MIDNIGHT

Select Codes from the main menu and enter MAVMID7.

MERCURIO

Select Codes from the main menu and enter RSMERC9.

SEMPER FIRE ULTRA

Select Codes from the main menu and enter CROMO1.

SPARTAN NCS-12

Select Codes from the main menu and enter THISIS12.

STAMPEDE

Select Codes from the main menu and enter DOGIE15.

VULCAN MAGMA

Select Codes from the main menu and enter MAGMA3.

NHL 2K9

3RD JERSEYS

At the codes menu enter R6y34bsH52.

NICKTOONS: ATTACK OF THE TOYBOTS

DAMAGE BOOST

Select Cheats from the Extras menu. Choose Enter Cheat Code and enter 456645.

INVULNERABILITY

Select Cheats from the Extras menu. Choose Enter Cheat Code and enter 313456.

UNLOCK EXO-HUGGLES 9000

Select Cheats from the Extras menu. Choose Enter Cheat Code and enter 691427.

UNLOCK MR. HUGGLES

Select Cheats from the Extras menu. Choose Enter Cheat Code and enter 654168.

UNLIMITED LOBBER GOO

Select Cheats from the Extras menu. Choose Enter Cheat Code and enter 118147.

UNLIMITED SCATTER GOO

Select Cheats from the Extras menu. Choose Enter Cheat Code and enter 971238.

UNLIMITED SPLITTER GOO

Select Cheats from the Extras menu. Choose Enter Cheat Code and enter 854511.

THE PRICE IS RIGHT 2010 EDITION

AVATAR UPGRADES

Select the lock tab from the Wardrobe screen and enter PRIZES.

PUNCH-OUT!!

REGAIN HEALTH BETWEEN ROUNDS

Press minus between rounds to regain health at the start of the next round.

DONKEY KONG IN EXHIBITION

Fight Donkey Kong in Last Stand mode.

CHAMPIONS MODE

Win 10 bouts in Mac's Last Stand.

RATATOUILLE

Select Gusteau's Shop from the Extras menu. Choose Secrets, select the appropriate code number, and then enter the code. Once the code is entered, select the cheat you want to activate it.

CODE NO.	CODE	EFFECT
1	Pieceocake	Very Easy difficulty mode
2	Myhero	No impact and no damage from enemies
3	Shielded	No damage from enemies
4	Spyagent	Move undetected by any enemy
5	Ilikeonions	Fart every time Remy jumps
6	Hardfeelings	Head butt when attacking instead of tailswipe
7	Slumberparty	Multiplayer mode
8	Gusteauart	All concept art
9	Gusteauship	All four championship modes
10	Mattelme	All single-player and multiplayer minigames
11	Gusteauvid	All videos
12	Gusteaures	All bonus artworks
13	Gusteaudream	All dream worlds in Gusteau's shop
14	Gusteauslide	All slides in Gusteau's shop
15	Gusteaulevel	All single-player minigames
16	Gusteaucombo	All items in Gusteau's shop
17	Gusteaupot	5,000 Gusteau points
18	Gusteaujack	10,000 Gusteau points
19	Gusteauomni	50,000 Gusteau points

RAYMAN RAVING RABBIDS 2

FUNKYTOWN

Play each game at least once.

RABBID COSTUMES

Costumes are unlocked as you score 12,000 points in certain games and when you shoot the correct rabbid in the shooting games.

COSTUME	MINIGAME	HOW TO UNLOCK
Cossack	Chess	Earn 12,000 points
Crash Test Dummy	Shopping Cart Downhill	Earn 12,000 points
Cupid	Burgerinnii	Earn 12,000 points
Doctor	Anesthetics	Earn 12,000 points
Fireman	Paris, Pour Troujours	Shoot fireman rabbid
French Maid	Little Chemist	Earn 12,000 points
Fruit-Hat Dancer	Year of the Rabbids	Shoot rabbid wearing fruit hat
Gingerbread	Hot Cake	Earn 12,000 points
HAZE Armor	Big City Fights	Shoot rabbid with armor
Indiana Jones	Rolling Stone	Earn 12,000 points
Jet Trooper	Greatest Hits	Earn 12,000 points
Ken	RRR Xtreme Beach Volleyball	Earn 12,000 points
Martian	Bumper Cars	Earn 12,000 points
Party Girl	Paris, Mon Amour	Once inside boat, shoot girl rabbid
Raider's	American Football	Earn 12,000 points
Sam Fisher	Rabbid School	Earn 12,000 points
Samurai	The Office	Earn 12,000 points
Space	Year of the Rabbids	Earn 12,000 points
Spider-	Spider Rabbid	Play the "Spider Rabbid" Game
TMNT, Leonardo	Usual Rabbids	Earn 12,000 points

COSTUME	MINIGAME	HOW TO UNLOCK
Transformer	Plumber Rabbids	Earn 12,000 points
Vegas Showgirl	Burp	Earn 12,000 points
Voodoo	Voodoo Rabbids	Earn 12,000 points
Wrestler	Greatest Hits	Shoot rabbid in green outfit

RUBIK'S PUZZLE WORLD

ALL LEVELS AND CUBIES

At the main menu, press A, B, B, A, A.

SCOOBY-DOO! FIRST FRIGHTS

DAPHNE'S SECRET COSTUME

Select Codes from the Extras menu and enter 2839.

FRED'S SECRET COSTUME

Select Codes from the Extras menu and enter 4826.

SCOOBY DOO'S SECRET COSTUME

Select Codes from the Extras menu and enter 1585.

SHAGGY'S SECRET COSTUME

Select Codes from the Extras menu and enter 3726.

VELMA'S SECRET COSTUME

Select Codes from the Extras menu and enter 6588.

SHREK THE THIRD

10,000 GOLD COINS
At the gift shop, press Up, Up, Down, Up, Right, Left.

THE SIMS 2: CASTAWAY

CHEAT GNOME
During a game, press B, Z, Up, Down, B. You can now use this Gnome to get the following:

MAX ALL MOTIVES
During a game, press Minus, Plus, Z, Z, A.

MAX CURRENT INVENTORY
During a game, press Left, Right, Left, Right, A.

MAX RELATIONSHIPS
During a game, press Z, Plus, A, B, 2.

ALL RESOURCES
During a game, press A, A, Down, Down, A.

ALL CRAFTING PLANS
During a game, press Plus, Plus, Minus, Minus, Z.

ADD 1 TO SKILL
During a game, press 2, Up, Right, Z, Right.

SIMANIMALS

FERRET
Begin a game in an unlocked forest area, press 2 to pause, and select Enter Codes. Enter Ferret.

PANDA
Begin a game in an unlocked forest area, press 2 to pause, and select Enter Codes. Enter PANDA.

RED PANDA
Begin a game in an unlocked forest area, press 2 to pause, and select Enter Codes. Enter Red Panda.

SIMCITY CREATOR

EGYPTIAN BUILDING SET
Name your city Mummy's desert.

GREEK BUILDING SET
Name your city Ancient culture.

JUNGLE BUILDING SET
Name your city Become wild.

SCI-FI BUILDING SET
Name your city Future picture.

THE SIMPSONS GAME

UNLIMITED POWER FOR ALL CHARACTERS
At the Extras menu, press Plus, Left, Right, Plus, Minus, Z.

ALL MOVIES
At the Extras menu, press Minus, Left, Minus, Right, Plus, C.

ALL CLICHÉS
At the Extras menu, press Left, Minus, Right, Plus, Right, Z.

SPACE HARRIER

CONTINUE AFTER GAME OVER

At the Game Over screen, press Up, Up, Down, Down, Left, Right, Left, Right, Down, Up, Down, Up.

SPECTROBES: ORIGINS

METALIC LEO AND RYZA

At the title screen, before creating a game save, press Up, Down, Left, Right, A.

SPEED RACER

INVULNERABILITY

Select Enter Code from the Options menu and enter A, B, A, Up, Left, Down, Right.

UNLIMITED BOOST

Select Enter Code from the Options menu and enter B, A, Down, Up, B, A, Down.

LAST 3 CARS

Select Enter Code from the Options menu and enter 1, 2, 1, 2, B, A, Plus.

GRANITE CAR

Select Enter Code from the Options menu and enter B, Up, Minus, Plus, 1, Up, Plus.

MONSTER TRUCK

Select Enter Code from the Options menu and enter B, Up, Minus, 2, B, Up, Minus.

AGGRESSIVE OPPONENTS

Select Enter Code from the Options menu and enter Up, Left, Down, Right, Up, Left, Down.

PACIFIST OPPONENTS

Select Enter Code from the Options menu and enter Up, Right, Down, Left, Up, Right, Down.

TINY OPPONENTS

Select Enter Code from the Options menu and enter B, A, Left, Down, Minus, Up, Minus.

HELIUM

Select Enter Code from the Options menu and enter Minus, Up, Minus, 2, Minus, Up, Minus.

MOON GRAVITY

Select Enter Code from the Options menu and enter Up, Plus, Up, Right, Minus, Up, Minus.

OVERKILL

Select Enter Code from the Options menu and enter A, Minus, Plus, Down, Up, Plus, 1.

PSYCHEDELIC

Select Enter Code from the Options menu and enter Left, A, Right, Down, B, Up, Minus.

SPIDER-MAN: FRIEND OR FOE

NEW GREEN GOBLIN AS A SIDEKICK

While standing in the Helicarrier between levels, press Left, Down, Right, Right, Down, Left.

SANDMAN AS A SIDEKICK

While standing in the Helicarrier between levels, press Right, Right, Right, Up, Down, Left.

VENOM AS A SIDEKICK

While standing in the Helicarrier between levels, press Left, Left, Right, Up, Down, Down.

5000 TECH TOKENS

While standing in the Helicarrier between levels, press Up, Up, Down, Down, Left, Right.

SPONGEBOB SQUAREPANTS FEATURING NICKTOONS: GLOBS OF DOOM

When entering the following codes, the order of the characters going down is: SpongeBob SquarePants, Nicolai Technus, Danny Phantom, Dib, Zim, Tlaloc, Tak, Beautiful Gorgeous, Jimmy Neutron, Plankton. These names are shortened to the first name in the following.

ATTRACT COINS

Using the Upgrade Machine on the bottom level of the lair, select "Input cheat codes here". Enter Tlaloc, Plankton, Danny, Plankton, Tak. Coins are attracted to you making them much easier to collect.

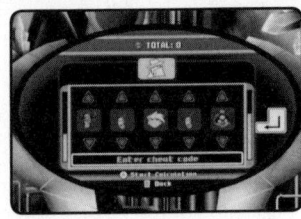

DON'T LOSE COINS

Using the Upgrade Machine on the bottom level of the lair, select "Input cheat codes here". Enter Plankton, Jimmy, Beautiful, Jimmy, Plankton. You don't lose coins when you get knocked out.

GOO HAS NO EFFECT

Using the Upgrade Machine on the bottom level of the lair, select "Input cheat codes here". Enter Danny, Danny, Danny, Nicolai, Nicolai. Goo does not slow you down.

MORE GADGET COMBO TIME

Using the Upgrade Machine on the bottom level of the lair, select "Input cheat codes here". Enter SpongeBob, Beautiful, Danny, Plankton, Nicolai. You have more time to perform gadget combos.

PATRICK TUX IN STARFISHMAN TO THE RESCUE

Select Cheat Codes from the Extras menu and enter PATRICK. Select Activate Bonus Items to enable this bonus item.

SPONGEBOB PLANKTON IN SUPER-SIZED PATTY

Select Cheat Codes from the Extras menu and enter PANTS. Select Activate Bonus Items to enable this bonus item.

PATRICK LASER COLOR IN ROCKET RODEO

Select Cheat Codes from the Extras menu and enter ROCKET. Select Activate Bonus Items to enable this bonus item.

PATRICK ROCKET SKIN COLOR IN ROCKET RODEO

Select Cheat Codes from the Extras menu and enter SPACE. Select Activate Bonus Items to enable this bonus item.

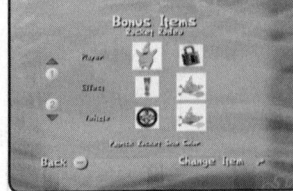

PLANKTON ASTRONAUT SUIT IN REVENGE OF THE GIANT PLANKTON MONSTER

Select Cheat Codes from the Extras menu and enter ROBOT. Select Activate Bonus Items to enable this bonus item.

PLANKTON EYE LASER COLOR IN REVENGE OF THE GIANT PLANKTON MONSTER

Select Cheat Codes from the Extras menu and enter LASER. Select Activate Bonus Items to enable this bonus item.

PIRATE PATRICK IN ROOFTOP RUMBLE

Select Cheat Codes from the Extras menu and enter PIRATE. Select Activate Bonus Items to enable this bonus item.

HOVERCRAFT VEHICLE SKIN IN HYPNOTIC HIGHWAY—PLANKTON

Select Cheat Codes from the Extras menu and enter HOVER. Select Activate Bonus Items to enable this bonus item.

STAR WARS: THE FORCE UNLEASHED

CHEATS

Once you have accessed the Rogue Shadow, select Enter Code from the Extras menu. Now you can enter the following codes:

CHEAT	CODE
Invincibility	CORTOSIS
Unlimited Force	VERGENCE
1,000,000 Force Points	SPEEDER
All Force Powers	TYRANUS
Max Force Power Level	KATARN
Max Combo Level	COUNTDOOKU
Stronger Lightsaber	LIGHTSABER

COSTUMES

Once you have accessed the Rogue Shadow, select Enter Code from the Extras menu. Now you can enter the following codes:

COSTUME	CODE	COSTUME	CODE
All Costumes	GRANDMOFF	Juno Eclipse	ECLIPSE
501st Legion	LEGION	Kento's Robe	WOOKIEE
Aayla Secura	AAYLA	Kleef	KLEEF
Admiral Ackbar	ITSATWAP	Lando Calrissian	SCOUNDREL
Anakin Skywalker	CHOSENONE	Luke Skywalker	T16WOMPRAT
Asajj Ventress	ACOLYTE	Luke Skywalker (Yavin)	YELLOWJCKT
Ceremonial Jedi Robes	DANTOOINE	Mace Windu	JEDIMASTER
Chop'aa Notimo	NOTIMO	Mara Jade	MARAJADE
Classic stormtrooper	TK421	Maris Brook	MARISBROOD
Count Dooku	SERENNO	Navy commando	STORMTROOP
Darth Desolous	PAUAN	Obi Wan Kenobi	BENKENOBI
Darth Maul	ZABRAK	Proxy	HOLOGRAM
Darth Phobos	HIDDENFEAR	Qui Gon Jinn	MAVERICK
Darth Vader	SITHLORD	Shaak Ti	TOGRUTA
Drexl Roosh	DREXLROOSH	Shadow trooper	INTHEDARK
Emperor Palpatine	PALPATINE	Sith Robes	HOLOCRON
General Rahm Kota	MANDALORE	Sith Stalker Armor	KORRIBAN
Han Solo	NERFHERDER	Twi'lek	SECURA
Heavy trooper	SHOCKTROOP		

STRONG BAD'S COOL GAME FOR ATTRACTIVE PEOPLE EPISODE 1: HOMESTAR RUINER

COBRA MODE IN SNAKE BOXER 5

At the Snake Boxer 5 title screen, press Up, Up, Down, Up, Plus.

SUPER C

RETAIN LIVES AND SCORE ON NEW GAME
After defeating the game, press A, Start.

RETAIN SCORE ON NEW GAME
After defeating the game, press A, B, Start.

10 LIVES
At the title screen press Right, Left, Down, Up, A, B, Start.

SOUND TEST
At the title screen hold A + B and press Start.

SUPER MARIO GALAXY

PLAY AS LUIGI
Collect all 120 stars and fight Bowser. After the credits you will get a message that Luigi is playable.

GRAND FINALE GALAXY
Collect all 120 stars with Luigi and beat Bowser.

STAR 121
Collect 100 purple coins.

SWORDS AND SOLDIERS

ALL LEVELS AND MODES
Pause the game and press Down, Up, B, Left, B, Up, Right, B.

10,000 MANA
Pause the game and press B, Left, Up, B, B, Left, Up, B.

10,000 MONEY
Pause the game and press Right, Up, B, B, B, Left, Up, Down.

LOSE LEVEL
Pause the game and press Down, Up, Left, Left, B, Up, Left, Left.

WIN LEVEL
Pause the game and press B, Right, Up, Left, B, Up, Left, Left.

TEENAGE MUTANT NINJA TURTLES: SMASH-UP

NINJA RABBID AND UNDERGROUND STAGE
At the Bonus Content menu, press Up, Up, Down, Down, Down, Right, Up, Left, Right, Left.

SHREDDER AND CYBER SHREDDER OUTFIT
At the Bonus Content menu, press Up, Down, Right, Up, Down, Right, Left, Up, Right, Down.

THRILLVILLE: OFF THE RAILS

$50,000
During a game, press C, Z, B, C, Z, B, A.

500 THRILL POINTS
During a game, press Z, C, B, Z, C, B, C.

ALL MISSIONS
During a game, press C, Z, B, C, Z, B, Z.

ALL PARKS
During a game, press C, Z, B, C, Z, B, C.

ALL RIDES
During a game, press C, Z, B, C, Z, B, B.

ALL MINIGAMES
During a game, press C, Z, B, C, Z, B, Right.

TIGER WOODS PGA TOUR 08

ALL CLUBS
Select Passwords from the Options and enter PROSHOP.

ALL GOLFERS
Select Passwords from the Options and enter GAMEFACE.

BRIDGESTONE ITEMS
Select Passwords from the Options and enter NOTJUSTTIRES.

BUICK ITEMS
Select Passwords from the Options and enter THREESTRIPES.

CLEVELAND GOLF ITEMS
Select Passwords from the Options and enter CLEVELAND.

COBRA ITEMS
Select Passwords from the Options and enter SNAKEKING.

EA ITEMS
Select Passwords from the Options and enter INTHEGAME.

GRAFALLOY ITEMS
Select Passwords from the Options and enter JUSTSHAFTS.

MIZUNO ITEMS
Select Passwords from the Options and enter RIHACHINRIZO.

NIKE ITEMS
Select Passwords from the Options and enter JUSTDOIT.

PRECEPT ITEMS
Select Passwords from the Options and enter GUYSAREGOOD.

TIGER WOODS PGA TOUR 09 ALL-PLAY

SPECTATORS BIG HEAD MODE
Select EA SPORTS Extras from My Tiger '09, choose Password and enter cephalus.

TIGER WOODS PGA TOUR 10

TW ITEMS IN PRO SHOP
Select Password from the Options and enter eltigre.

TONY HAWK'S PROVING GROUND

Select Cheat Codes from the Options and enter the following cheats. Some codes need to be enabled by selecting Cheats from the Options during a game.

UNLOCK	CHEAT	UNLOCK	CHEAT
Unlocks Bosco	MOREMILK	Unlocks Shayne	MOVERS
Unlocks Cam	NOTACAMERA	Unlocks TV Producer	SHAKER
Unlocks Cooper	THECOOP	Unlock FDR	THEPREZPARK
Unlocks Eddie X	SKETCHY	Unlock Lansdowne	THELOCALPARK
Unlocks El Patinador	PILEDRIVER	Unlock Air & Space Museum	THEINDOORPARK
Unlocks Eric	FLYAWAY	Unlocks all Fun Items	OVERTHETOP
Unlocks Judy Nails	LOVEROCKNROLL	Unlock all Game Movies	WATCHTHIS
Unlocks Mad Dog	RABBIES	Unlock all Rigger Pieces	IMGONNABUILD
Unlocks MCA	INTERGALACTIC	All specials unlocked and in player's special list	LOTSOFTRICKS
Unlocks Mel	NOTADUDE	Full Stats	BEEFEDUP
Unlocks Rube	LOOKSSMELLY	Give player +50 skill points	NEEDSHELP
Unlocks Spence	DAPPER		

The following cheats lock you out of the Leaderboards:

Unlocks Perfect Manual	STILLAINTFALLIN
Unlocks Perfect Rail	AINTFALLIN
Unlocks Unlimited Focus	MYOPIC

You cannot use the Video Editor with the following cheats:

Invisible Man	THEMISSING
Mini Skater	TINYTATER

TRANSFORMERS: THE GAME

INFINITE HEALTH

At the Main menu, press Left, Left, Up, Left, Right, Down, Right.

INFINITE AMMO

At the Main menu, press Up, Down, Left, Right, Up, Up, Down.

NO MILITARY OR POLICE

At the Main menu, press Right, Left, Right, Left, Right, Left, Right.

ALL MISSIONS

At the Main menu, press Down, Up, Left, Right, Right, Right, Up, Down.

BONUS CYBERTRON MISSIONS

At the Main menu, press Right, Up, Up, Down, Right, Left, Left.

GENERATION 1 SKIN: JAZZ

At the Main menu, press Left, Up, Down, Down, Left, Up, Right.

GENERATION 1 SKIN: MEGATRON

At the Main menu, press Down, Left, Left, Down, Right, Right, Up.

GENERATION 1 SKIN: OPTIMUS PRIME

At the Main menu, press Down, Right, Left, Up, Down, Down, Left.

GENERATION 1 SKIN: ROBOVISION OPTIMUS PRIME

At the Main menu, press Down, Down, Up, Up, Right, Right, Right.

GENERATION 1 SKIN: STARSCREAM

At the Main menu, press Right, Down, Left, Left, Down, Up, Up.

ULTIMATE SHOOTING COLLECTION

ROTATE DISPLAY ON SIDE IN TATE MODE

At the main menu, press Left, Right, Left, Right, Up, Up, 1, 2.

WALL-E

The following cheats will disable saving. The five possible characters starting with Wall-E and going down are: Wall-E, Auto, EVE, M-O, GEL-A Steward.

ALL BONUS FEATURES UNLOCKED

Select Cheats from the Bonus Features menu and enter Wall-E, Auto, EVE, GEL-A Steward.

ALL GAME CONTENT UNLOCKED

Select Cheats from the Bonus Features menu and enter M-O, Auto, GEL-A Steward, EVE.

ALL SINGLE-PLAYER LEVELS UNLOCKED

Select Cheats from the Bonus Features menu and enter Auto, GEL-A Steward, M-O, Wall-E.

ALL MULTIPLAYER MAPS UNLOCKED

Select Cheats from the Bonus Features menu and enter EVE, M-O, Wall-E, Auto.

ALL HOLIDAY COSTUMES UNLOCKED

Select Cheats from the Bonus Features menu and enter Auto, Auto, GEL-A Steward, GEL-A Steward.

ALL MULTIPLAYER COSTUMES UNLOCKED

Select Cheats from the Bonus Features menu and enter GEL-A Steward, Wall-E, M-O, Auto.

UNLIMITED HEALTH UNLOCKED

Select Cheats from the Bonus Features menu and enter Wall-E, M-O, Auto, M-O.

WALL-E: MAKE ANY CUBE AT ANY TIME

Select Cheats from the Bonus Features menu and enter Auto, M-O, Auto, M-O.

WALL-EVE: MAKE ANY CUBE AT ANY TIME

Select Cheats from the Bonus Features menu and enter M-O, GEL-A Steward, EVE, EVE.

WALL-E WITH A LASER GUN AT ANY TIME

Select Cheats from the Bonus Features menu and enter Wall-E, EVE, EVE, Wall-E.

WALL-EVE WITH A LASER GUN AT ANY TIME

Select Cheats from the Bonus Features menu and enter GEL-A Steward, EVE, M-O, Wall-E.

WALL-E: PERMANENT SUPER LASER UPGRADE

Select Cheats from the Bonus Features menu and enter Wall-E, Auto, EVE, M-O.

EVE: PERMANENT SUPER LASER UPGRADE

Select Cheats from the Bonus Features menu and enter EVE, Wall-E, Wall-E, Auto.

CREDITS

Select Cheats from the Bonus Features menu and enter Auto, Wall-E, GEL-A Steward, M-O.

WII SPORTS

BOWLING BALL COLOR

After selecting your Mii, hold the following direction on the D-pad and press A at the warning screen:

DIRECTION	COLOR
Up	Blue
Right	Gold
Down	Green
Left	Red

NO HUD IN GOLF

Hold 2 as you select a course to disable the power meter, map, and wind speed meter.

BLUE TENNIS COURT

After selecting your Mii, hold 2 and press A at the warning screen.

WII SPORTS RESORT

MODIFY EVENTS

At the Select a Mii screen, hold 2 while pressing A while on "OK." This will make the following modifications to each event.

EVENT	MODIFICATION
Air Sports Island Flyover	No balloons or I points
Air Sports Skydiving	Play intro event
Archery	More difficult; no aiming reticule
Basketball Pickup Game	Nighttime
Frisbee Golf	No wind display or distance
Golf	No wind display or distance
Swordplay Duel	Evening
Table Tennis Match	11-point match

WWE SMACKDOWN VS. RAW 2010

THE ROCK

Select Cheat Codes from the Options and enter The Great One.

VINCE'S OFFICE AND DIRT SHEET FOR BACKSTAGE BRAWL

Select Cheat Codes from the Options menu and enter BonusBrawl.

Nintendo Wii™: Virtual Console

For the Virtual Console games, a Classic Controller may be needed to enter some codes.

ALTERED BEAST

LEVEL SELECT

At the Title screen, press B + Start.

BEAST SELECT

At the Title screen, hold A + B + C + Down/Left and press Start.

SOUND TEST

At the Title screen, hold A + C + Up/Right and press Start.

CHEW MAN FU

GAME COMPLETE PASSWORDS

Select Password and enter 573300 or 441300.

COMIX ZONE

STAGE SELECT

At the Jukebox menu, press C on the following numbers:

14, 15, 18, 5, 13, 1, 3, 18, 15, 6

A voice says "Oh Yeah" when entered correctly. Then, press C on 1 through 6 to warp to that stage.

INVINCIBLE

At the Jukebox menu, press C on the following numbers:

3, 12, 17, 2, 2, 10, 2, 7, 7, 11

A voice says "Oh Yeah" when entered correctly.

CREDITS

At the Options menu press A + B + C.

DR. ROBOTNIK'S MEAN BEAN MACHINE

EASY PASSWORDS

STAGE	PASSWORD
02: Frankly	Red Bean, Red Bean, Red Bean, Has Bean
03: Humpty	Clear Bean, Purple Bean, Clear Bean, Green Bean
04: Coconuts	Red Bean, Clear Bean, Has Bean, Yellow Bean
05: Davy Sprocket	Clear Bean, Blue Bean, Blue Bean, Purple Bean
06: Skweel	Clear Bean, Red Bean, Clear Bean, Purple Bean

STAGE	PASSWORD
07: Dynamight	Purple Bean, Yellow Bean, Red Bean, Blue Bean
08: Grounder	Yellow Bean, Purple Bean, Has Bean, Blue Bean
09: Spike	Yellow Bean, Purple Bean, Has Bean, Blue Bean
10: Sir Ffuzy-Logik	Red Bean, Yellow Bean, Clear Bean, Has Bean
11: Dragon Breath	Green Bean, Purple Bean, Blue Bean, Clear Bean
12: Scratch	Red Bean, Has Bean, Has Bean, Yellow Bean
13: Dr. Robotnik	Yellow Bean, Has Bean, Blue Bean, Blue Bean

NORMAL PASSWORDS

STAGE	PASSWORD
02: Frankly	Has Bean, Clear Bean, Yellow Bean, Yellow Bean
03: Humpty	Blue Bean, Clear Bean, Red Bean, Yellow Bean
04: Coconuts	Yellow Bean, Blue Bean, Clear Bean, Purple Bean
05: Davy Sprocket	Has Bean, Green Bean, Blue Bean, Yellow Bean
06: Skweel	Green Bean, Purple Bean, Purple Bean, Yellow Bean
07: Dynamight	Purple Bean, Blue Bean, Green Bean, Has Bean
08: Grounder	Green Bean, Has Bean, Clear Bean, Yellow Bean
09: Spike	Blue Bean, Purple Bean, Has Bean, Has Bean
10: Sir Ffuzy-Logik	Has Bean, Red Bean, Yellow Bean, Clear Bean
11: Dragon Breath	Clear Bean, Red Bean, Red Bean, Blue Bean
12: Scratch	Green Bean, Green Bean, Clear Bean, Yellow Bean
13: Dr. Robotnik	Purple Bean, Yellow Bean, Has Bean, Clear Bean

HARD PASSWORDS

STAGE	PASSWORD
02: Frankly	Clear Bean, Green Bean, Yellow Bean, Yellow Bean
03: Humpty	Yellow Bean, Purple Bean, Clear Bean, Purple Bean
04: Coconuts	Blue Bean, Green Bean, Clear Bean, Blue Bean
05: Davy Sprocket	Red Bean, Purple Bean, Green Bean, Green Bean
06: Skweel	Yellow Bean, Yellow Bean, Clear Bean, Green Bean
07: Dynamight	Purple Bean, Clear Bean, Blue Bean, Blue Bean
08: Grounder	Clear Bean, Yellow Bean, Has Bean, Yellow Bean
09: Spike	Purple Bean, Blue Bean, Blue Bean, Green Bean
10: Sir Ffuzy-Logik	Clear Bean, Green Bean, Red Bean, Yellow Bean
11: Dragon Breath	Blue Bean, Yellow Bean, Yellow Bean, Has Bean
12: Scratch	Green Bean, Clear Bean, Clear Bean, Blue Bean
13: Dr. Robotnik	Has Bean, Clear Bean, Purple Bean, Has Bean

HARDEST PASSWORDS

STAGE	PASSWORD
02: Frankly	Blue Bean, Blue Bean, Green Bean, Yellow Bean
03: Humpty	Green Bean, Yellow Bean, Green Bean, Clear Bean
04: Coconuts	Purple Bean, Purple Bean, RedBean, Has Bean
05: Davy Sprocket	Green Bean, Red Bean, Purple Bean, Blue Bean
06: Skweel	Purple Bean, Clear Bean, Green Bean, Yellow Bean
07: Dynamight	Blue Bean, Purple Bean, Green Bean, Has Bean
08: Grounder	Clear Bean, Purple Bean, Yellow Bean, Has Bean
09: Spike	Purple Bean, Green Bean, Has Bean, Clear Bean
10: Sir Ffuzy-Logik	Green Bean, Blue Bean, Yellow Bean, Has Bean
11: Dragon Breath	Green Bean, Purple Bean, Has Bean, Red Bean
12: Scratch	Red Bean, Green Bean, Has Bean, Blue Bean
13: Dr. Robotnik	Red Bean, Red Bean, Clear Bean, Yellow Bean

ECCO THE DOLPHIN

DEBUG MENU

Pause the game with Ecco facing the screen and press Right, B, C, B, C, Down, C, Up.

INFINITE AIR

Enter LIFEFISH as a password.

PASSWORDS

LEVEL	PASSWORD	LEVEL	PASSWORD
The Undercaves	WEFIDNMP	Deep City	DDXPQQLJ
The Vents	BQDPXJDS	City of Forever	MSDBRQLA
The Lagoon	JNSBRIKY	Jurassic Beach	IYCBUNLB
Ridge Water	NTSBZTKB	Pteranodon Pond	DMXEUNLI
Open Ocean	YWGTTJNI	Origin Beach	EGRIUNLB
Ice Zone	HZIFZBMF	Trilobite Circle	IELMUNLB
Hard Water	LRFJRQLI	Dark Water	RKEQUNLN
Cold Water	UYNFRQLC	City of Forever 2	HPQIGPLA
Island Zone	LYTIOQLZ	The Tube	JUMFKMLB
Deep Water	MNOPOQLR	The Machine	GXUBKMLF
The Marble	RJNTQQLZ	The Last Fight	TSONLMLU
The Library	RTGXQQLE		

F-ZERO X

ALL TRACKS, VEHICLES, AND DIFFICULTIES

At the Mode Select screen, press Up on the D-pad, L, R, Up on the Right control stick, X, Y, ZR, Plus.

GOLDEN AXE

LEVEL SELECT

At the Character Select screen, in Arcade mode, hold Down/Left and press B + Start.

START WITH 9 CONTINUES

At the Character Select screen, in Arcade mode, hold Down/Left and then hold A + C. Release the buttons and select a character.

GRADIUS

MAX OUT WEAPONS

Pause the game and press Up, Up, Down, Down, Left, Right, Left, Right, B, A.

GRADIUS III

FULL POWER-UP

Pause the game and press Up, Up, Down, Down, L, R, L, R, B, A.

SUICIDE

Pause the game and press Up, Up, Down, Down, Left, Right, Left, Right, B, A.

MILITARY MADNESS

PASSWORDS

LEVEL	PASSWORD	LEVEL	PASSWORD
01	REVOLT	04	RAMSEY
02	ICARUS	05	NEWTON
03	CYRANO	06	SENECA

LEVEL	PASSWORD	LEVEL	PASSWORD
07	SABINE	20	INAKKA
08	ARATUS	21	TETROS
09	GALIOS	22	ARBINE
10	DARWIN	23	RECTOS
11	PASCAL	24	YEANTA
12	HALLEY	25	MONOGA
13	BORMAN	26	ATTAYA
14	APOLLO	27	DESHTA
15	KAISER	28	NEKOSE
16	NECTOR	29	ERATIN
17	MILTON	30	SOLCIS
18	IRAGAN	31	SAGINE
19	LIPTUS	32	WINNER

SOUND TEST

Enter ONGAKU as a password.

RISTAR

Select Passwords from the Options menu and enter the following:

LEVEL SELECT
ILOVEU

BOSS RUSH MODE
MUSEUM

TIME ATTACK MODE
DOFEEL

TOUGHER DIFFICULTY
SUPER

ONCHI MUSIC
MAGURO. Activate this from the Sound Test.

CLEARS PASSWORD
XXXXXX

GAME COPYRIGHT INFO
AGES

SONIC THE HEDGEHOG

LEVEL SELECT

At the Title screen, press Up, Down, Left, Right. A sound of a ring being collected plays if the code is entered correctly. Hold A and press Start to access the Level Select.

CONTROL MODE

At the Title screen, press Up, C, Down, C, Left, C, Right, C. Then, hold A and press Start.

DEBUG MODE

After entering the Control Mode, hold A and press Start. Press A to change Sonic into another sprite. Press B to change back to Sonic. Press C to place that sprite. Pause the game and press A to restart. Hold B for slow motion and press C to advance a frame.

CHANGE DEMO

During the demo, hold C and Sonic will start making mistakes.

WARIO'S WOODS

HARD BATTLES

Highlight VS. Computer Mode, hold Left and press Start.

XBOX 360™

TABLE OF CONTENTS

AMPED 3

ALL SLEDS

Select Cheat Codes from the Options screen and press Right Trigger, ❌, Left Trigger, Down, Right, Left Bumper, Left Trigger, Right Trigger, ⓨ, ❌.

ALL GEAR

Select Cheat Codes from the Options and press ⓨ, Down, Up, Left, Right, Left Bumper, Right, Right Trigger, Right Trigger, Right Bumper.

ALL TRICKS

Select Cheat Codes from the Options screen and press Left Bumper, Right Trigger, Ⓨ, Up, Down, Ⓧ, Left Trigger, Left, Right Bumper, Right Trigger.

ALL LEVELS

Select Cheat Codes from the Options screen and press Ⓧ, Ⓨ, Up, Left, Left Bumper, Left Bumper, Right Trigger, Ⓧ, Ⓨ, Left Trigger.

ALL CONFIGS

Select Cheat Codes from the Options screen and press Down, Ⓧ, Right, Left Bumper, Right, Right Bumper, Ⓧ, Right Trigger, Left Trigger, Ⓨ.

SUPER SPINS

Select Cheat Codes from the Options screen and press Ⓧ(x4), Ⓨ(x3), Ⓧ.

AWESOME METER ALWAYS FULL

Select Cheat Codes from the Options screen and press Up, Right Trigger, Ⓧ, Ⓨ Left Bumper, Ⓧ, Down, Left Bumper, Right Trigger, Right Bumper.

ALL AWESOMENESS

Select Cheat Codes from the Options screen and press Right Bumper, Right Bumper, Down, Left, Up, Right Trigger, Ⓧ, Right Bumper, Ⓧ, Ⓧ.

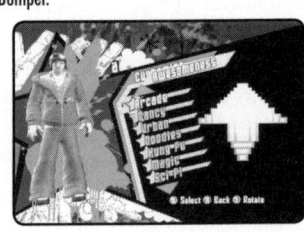

ALL BUILD LICENSES

Select Cheat Codes from the Options screen and press Left, Right Trigger, Left Bumper, Right Trigger, Ⓧ, Ⓧ, Ⓨ, Down, Up, Ⓧ.

ALL BUILD OBJECTS

Select Cheat Codes from the Options screen and press Left Trigger, Right Trigger, Up, Up, Right Bumper, Left, Right, Ⓧ, Ⓨ, Left Bumper.

ALL CHALLENGES

Select Cheat Codes from the Options screen and press Right, Left Bumper, Left Trigger, Ⓧ, Left, Right Bumper, Right Trigger, Ⓨ, Left Trigger, Ⓧ.

LOUD SPEAKERS

Select Cheat Codes from the Options screen and press Ⓨ. Right Trigger, Right Trigger, Left Bumper, Down, Down, Left, Left, Right, Left Bumper.

LOW GRAVITY BOARDERS

Select Cheat Codes from the Options screen and press Right Trigger, Down, Down, Up, Ⓧ, Left Bumper, Ⓨ, Right Trigger, Ⓨ, Down.

NO AI

Select Cheat Codes from the Options screen and press ✖, ✖, Left Bumper, Down, Right, Right, Up, ▼, ▼, Left Trigger.

ALL MUSIC

Select Cheat Codes from the Options screen and press Up, Left, Right Trigger, Right Bumper, Right Trigger, Up, Down, Left, ▼, Left Trigger.

AVATAR: THE LAST AIRBENDER - THE BURNING EARTH

UNLIMITED HEALTH

Select Code Entry from the Extras menu and enter 65049.

DOUBLE DAMAGE

Select Code Entry from the Extras menu and enter 90210.

MAXIMUM LEVEL

Select Code Entry from the Extras menu and enter 89121.

UNLIMITED SPECIALS

Select Code Entry from the Extras menu and enter 66206.

ONE-HIT DISHONOR

Select Code Entry from the Extras menu and enter 28260.

ALL BONUS GAMES

Select Code Entry from the Extras menu and enter 99801.

UNLOCKS GALLERY

Select Code Entry from the Extras menu and enter 85061.

BAJA: EDGE OF CONTROL

ALL VEHICLES AND TRACKS

Select Cheat Codes from the Options menu and enter SHOWTIME.

ALL PARTS

Select Cheat Codes from the Options menu and enter SUPERMAX.

BANJO-KAZOOIE

In Treasure Trove Cove, enter the Sandcastle and spell CHEAT by using your Beak Buster on the desired letter. A sound will confirm the entry of the letter. The following cheats will now be available for you. Two things to keep in mind. The first is that no sound will confirm the correct letter. Secondly, ignore the spaces in the phrases…just spell the entire phrase out.

AREA OPENING CHEATS

ACCESS CLANKER'S CAVERN

THERES NOWHERE DANKER THAN IN WITH CLANKER

ACCESS MAD MONSTER MANSION

THE JIGGYS NOW MADE WHOLE INTO THE MANSION YOU CAN STROLL

ACCESS GOBI'S VALLEY

GOBIS JIGGY IS NOW DONE TREK ON IN AND GET SOME SUN

ACCESS RUSTY BUCKET BAY
WHY NOT TAKE A TRIP INSIDE GRUNTYS RUSTY SHIP

ACCESS CLICK CLOCK WOOD
THIS ONES GOOD AS YOU CAN ENTER THE WOOD

ACCESS FREEZEEZY PEAK
THE JIGGYS DONE SO OFF YOU GO INTO FREEZEEZY PEAK AND ITS SNOW

ACCESS BUBBLEGLOOP SWAMP
NOW INTO THE SWAMP YOU CAN STOMP

HIDDEN EGG CHEATS
The Hidden Egg cheats will only work if you have been to the level previously.

REVEAL THE BLUE EGG IN GOBI'S VALLEY BEHIND THE LOCKED GATE IN THE ROCK WALL
A DESERT DOOR OPENS WIDE ANCIENT SECRETS WAIT INSIDE

REVEAL THE PURPLE EGG IN TREASURE TROVE COVE IN SHARKFOOD ISLAND
OUT OF THE SEA IT RISES TO REVEAL MORE SECRET PRIZES

REVEAL THE ICE KEY IN FREEZEEZY PEAK IN THE ICE CAVE
NOW YOU CAN SEE A NICE ICE KEY WHICH YOU CAN HAVE FOR FREE

REVEAL THE LIGHT BLUE EGG IN GRUNTILDA'S LAIR–YOU'LL FIND IT IN THE CASK MARKED WITH AN X
DONT YOU GO AND TELL HER ABOUT THE SECRET IN HER CELLAR

REVEAL THE GREEN EGG IN MAD MONSTER MANSION IN THE SAME ROOM AS LOGGO THE TOILET
AMIDST THE HAUNTED GLOOM A SECRET IN THE BATHROOM

REVEAL THE YELLOW EGG IN CLICK CLOCK WOOD IN NABNUTS' TREE HOUSE
NOW BANJO WILL BE ABLE TO SEE IT ON NABNUTS TABLE

REVEAL THE RED EGG IN RUSTY BUCKET BAY IN THE CAPTAIN'S CABIN
THIS SECRET YOULL BE GRABBIN IN THE CAPTAINS CABIN

NOTE DOOR CHEATS
These will pop those note doors open without having to find the required notes.

DOOR 2
THESE GO RIGHT ON THROUGH NOTE DOOR TWO

DOOR 3
NOTE DOOR THREE GET IN FOR FREE

DOOR 4
TAKE A TOUR THROUGH NOTE DOOR FOUR

DOOR 5
USE THIS CHEAT NOTE DOOR FIVE IS BEAT

DOOR 6
THIS TRICKS USED TO OPEN NOTE DOOR SIX

DOOR 7
THE SEVENTH NOTE DOOR IS NOW NO MORE

SWITCH AND OBSTACLE CHEATS FOR GRUNTILDA'S LAIR

These will allow you to alter certain obstacles throughout Gruntilda's Lair. Sometimes, the cheat will even remove them completely.

RAISE THE PIPES NEAR CLANKER'S CAVERN
BOTH PIPES ARE THERE TO CLANKE⊛ LAIR

RAISE THE LARGE PIPE NEAR CLANKER'S CAVERN:
YOULL CEASE TO GRIPE WHEN UP GOES A PIPE

UNLOCK THE PATH NEAR CLANKER'S CAVERN THAT LEADS TO THE CLICK CLOCK WOOD PICTURE
ONCE IT SHONE BUT THE LONG TUNNEL GRILLE IS GONE

REVEAL THE PODIUM FOR THE CLICK CLOCK WOOD JIGGY
DONT DESPAIR THE TREE JIGGY PODIUM IS NOW THERE

UNLOCK THE PATH INSIDE THE GIANT WITCH STATUE, NEAR BUBBLEGLOOP SWAMP (OPEN THE GRILL)
SHES AN UGLY BAT SO LETS REMOVE HER GRILLE AND HAT

UNLOCK THE PATH TO THE FREEZEEZY PEAK PICTURE BEHIND THE ICE CUBE
ITS YOUR LUCKY DAY AS THE ICE BALL MELTS AWAY

UNLOCK PASSAGES BLOCKED BY COBWEBS
WEBS STOP YOUR PLAY SO TAKE THEM AWAY

REVEAL A JIGGY IN GRUNTILDA'S STATUE BY SMASHING THE EYE NEAR MAD MONSTER MANSION
GRUNTY WILL CRY NOW YOUVE SMASHED HER EYE

RAISE THE WATER LEVEL NEAR RUSTY BUCKET BAY
UP YOU GO WITHOUT A HITCH UP TO THE WATER LEVEL SWITCH

UNLOCK THE PATH TO THE CRYPT NEAR MAD MONSTER MANSION (REMOVE THE GATE)
YOU WONT HAVE TO WAIT NOW THERES NO CRYPT GATE

REMOVE THE COFFIN LID IN THE CRYPT
THIS SHOULD GET RID OF THE CRYPT COFFIN LID

CRUMBLE ALL BREAKABLE WALLS
THEY CAUSE TROUBLE BUT NOW THEYRE RUBBLE

ACTIVATE SPECIAL PADS

Skip the lesson from Bottles by entering these codes.

ACTIVATE THE FLY PAD
YOU WONT BE SAD NOW YOU CAN USE THE FLY PAD

ACTIVATE THE SHOCK JUMP PAD
YOULL BE GLAD TO SEE THE SHOCK JUMP PAD

EXTRA HEALTH CHEAT

Skip the note-hunt and get that extra health by entering this cheat.

AN ENERGY BAR TO GET YOU FAR

Remember, to enter a code you must first enter the word CHEAT in the Sandcastle.

BANJO-TOOIE

REGAIN ENERGY

Go to the Code Chamber in the Mayahem Temple and access the scroll on the wall.
If you have been awarded this cheat by Cheato, enter HONEYBACK. If not, enter
CHEATOKCABYENOH.

FALLS DON'T HURT

Go to the Code Chamber in the Mayahem Temple and access the scroll on the wall. If you
have been awarded this cheat by Cheato, enter FALLPROOF. If not, enter CHEATOFOORPLLAF.

HOMING EGGS

Go to the Code Chamber in the Mayahem Temple and access the scroll on the wall. If you
have been awarded this cheat, enter HOMING. If not, enter CHEATOGNIMOH.

DOUBLES MAXIMUM EGGS

Go to the Code Chamber in the Mayahem Temple and access the scroll on the wall. If you
have been awarded this cheat by Cheato, enter EGGS. If not, enter CHEATOSGGE.

DOUBLES MAXIMUM FEATHERS

Go to the Code Chamber in the Mayahem Temple and access the scroll on the wall. If you
have been awarded this cheat by Cheato, enter FEATHE❂. If not, enter CHEATOSREHTAEF.

JOLLY ROGER LAGOON'S JUKEBOX

Go to the Code Chamber in the Mayahem Temple and access the scroll on the wall. If you
have been awarded this cheat, enter JUKEBOX. If not, enter CHEATOXOBEKUJ.

SIGNS IN JIGGYWIGGY'S TEMPLE GIVE HINTS TO GET EACH JIGGY

Go to the Code Chamber in the Mayahem Temple and access the scroll on the wall. If you
have been awarded this cheat, enter GETJIGGY. If not, enter CHEATOYGGIJTEG.

ALL LEVELS

Go to the Code Chamber in the Mayahem Temple and enter JIGGYWIGGYSPECIAL.

SPEED BANJO

Go to the Code Chamber in the Mayahem Temple and enter SUPE🔳ANJO.

SPEED ENEMIES

Go to the Code Chamber in the Mayahem Temple and enter SUPE🔳ADDY.

INFINITE EGGS AND FEATHERS

Go to the Code Chamber in the Mayahem Temple and enter NESTKING.

INFINITE HONEY

Go to the Code Chamber in the Mayahem Temple and enter HONEYKING.

BATTLESTATIONS: MIDWAY

ALL CAMPAIGN AND CHALLENGE MISSIONS

At the mission select, hold Right Bumper + Left Bumper + Right Trigger + Left Trigger and
press ❌.

BEAT'N GROOVY

ALTERNATE CONTROLS

At the title screen, press Up, Up, Down, Down, Left, Right, Left, Right, Ⓑ, Ⓐ.

BLAZING ANGELS: SQUADRONS OF WWII

ALL MISSIONS, MEDALS, & PLANES

At the Main menu hold Left Trigger +
Right Trigger and press ⊗, Left Bumper,
Right Bumper, ⓨ, ⓨ Right Bumper, Left
Bumper, ⊗.

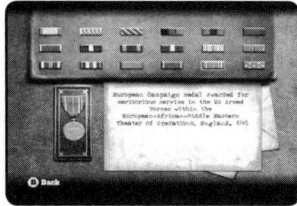

GOD MODE

Pause the game, hold Left Trigger and press
⊗, ⓨ, ⓨ, ⊗ Release Left Trigger, hold
Right Trigger and press ⓨ, ⊗, ⊗, ⓨ.
Re-enter the code to disable it.

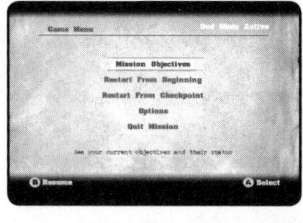

INCREASED DAMAGE

Pause the game, hold Left Trigger and press
Left Bumper, Left Bumper, Right Bumper.

Release Left Trigger, hold Right Trigger and press Right Bumper, Right Bumper, Left Bumper.
Re-enter the code to disable it.

BLAZING ANGELS 2: SECRET MISSIONS OF WWII

Achievements are disabled when using these codes.

ALL MISSIONS AND PLANES UNLOCKED

At the Main menu, hold Left Trigger + Right Trigger, and press ⊗, Left Bumper, Right
Bumper, ⓨ, ⓨ, Right Bumper, Left Bumper, ⊗.

GOD MODE

Pause the game, hold Left Trigger, and press ⊗, ⓨ, ⓨ, ⊗. Release Left Trigger, hold Right
Trigger and press ⓨ, ⊗, ⊗, ⓨ. Re-enter the code to disable it.

INCREASED DAMAGE WITH ALL WEAPONS

Pause the game, hold Left Trigger, and press Left Bumper, Left Bumper, Right Bumper.
Release Left Trigger, hold Right Trigger, and press Right Bumper, Right Bumper, Left Bumper.
Re-enter the code to disable it.

BURNOUT PARADISE

BEST BUY CAR

Pause the game and select Sponsor Product Code from the Under the Hood menu. Enter Bestbuy. Need A License to use this car offline.

CIRCUIT CITY CAR

Pause the game and select Sponsor Product Code from the Under the Hood menu. Enter Circuitcity. Need Burnout Paradise License to use this car offline.

GAMESTOP CAR

Pause the game and select Sponsor Product Code from the Under the Hood menu. Enter Gamestop. Need A License to use this car offline.

WALMART CAR

Pause the game and select Sponsor Product Code from the Under the Hood menu. Enter Walmart. Need Burnout Paradise License to use this car offline.

"STEEL WHEELS" GT

Pause the game and select Sponsor Product Code from the Under the Hood menu. Enter G23X 5K8Q GX2V 04B1 or E60J 8Z7T MS8L 51U6.

LICENSES

LICENSE	NUMBER OF WINS NEEDED
D	2
C	7
B	16
A	26
Burnout Paradise	45
Elite License	All events

CARS

UNLOCK EVERYTHING

Select Cheat Codes from the Options and enter IF900HP.

ALL CHARACTERS

Select Cheat Codes from the Options and enter YAYCA ⊕.

ALL CHARACTER SKINS

Select Cheat Codes from the Options and enter R4MONE.

ALL MINI-GAMES AND COURSES

Select Cheat Codes from the Options and enter MATTL66.

FAST START

Select Cheat Codes from the Options and enter IMSPEED.

INFINITE BOOST

Select Cheat Codes from the Options and enter VROOOOM.

ART

Select Cheat Codes from the Options and enter CONC3PT.

VIDEOS

Select Cheat Codes from the Options and enter WATCHIT.

CARS MATER-NATIONAL

ALL ARCADE RACES, MINI-GAMES, AND WORLDS

Select Codes/Cheats from the options and enter PLAYALL.

ALL CARS

Select Codes/Cheats from the options and enter MATTEL07.

ALTERNATE LIGHTNING MCQUEEN COLORS

Select Codes/Cheats from the options and enter NCEDUDZ.

ALL COLORS FOR OTHERS

Select Codes/Cheats from the options and enter PAINTIT.

UNLIMITED TURBO

Select Codes/Cheats from the options and enter ZZOOOOM.

EXTREME ACCELERATION

Select Codes/Cheats from the options and enter 0T0200X.

EXPERT MODE

Select Codes/Cheats from the options and enter VRYFAST.

ALL BONUS ART

Select Codes/Cheats from the options and enter BUYTALL.

CASTLEVANIA: SYMPHONY OF THE NIGHT

Before using the following codes, complete the game with 170%.

PLAY AS RICHTER BELMONT

Enter RICHTER as your name.

ALUCARD WITH AXELORD ARMOR

Enter AXEARMOR as your name.

ALUCARD WITH 99 LUCK AND OTHER STATS ARE LOW

Enter X-X!V"Q as your name.

CRASH BANDICOOT: MIND OVER MUTANT

A cheat can be deactivated by re-entering the code.

FREEZE ENEMIES WITH TOUCH

Pause the game, hold Right Trigger and press Down, Down, Down, Up.

ENEMIES DROP X4 DAMAGE

Pause the game, hold Right Trigger and press Up, Up, Up, Left.

ENEMIES DROP PURPLE FRUIT

Pause the game, hold Right Trigger and press Up, Down, Down, Up.

ENEMIES DROP SUPER KICK

Pause the game, hold Right Trigger and press Up, Right, Down, Left.

ENIMIES DROP WUMPA FRUIT

Pause the game, hold Right Trigger and press Right, Right, Right, Up.

SHADOW CRASH

Pause the game, hold Right Trigger and press Left, Right, Left, Right.

DEFORMED CRASH

Pause the game, hold Right Trigger and press Left, Left, Left, Down.

CRASH OF THE TITANS

BIG HEAD CRASH

Pause the game, hold the Right Trigger, and press ✖, ✖, Ⓨ, Ⓐ.

SHADOW CRASH

Pause the game, hold the Right Trigger, and press Ⓨ, ✖, Ⓨ, Ⓐ.

DEFENSE GRID: THE AWAKENING

The following cheats will disable Achievements.

100,000 RESOURCES

Click and hold the Right Thumbstick and press Right, Right, Right, Right

CORES CANNOT BE TAKEN

Click and hold the Right Thumbstick and press Up, Left, Down, Right

FREE CAMERA MODE

Click and hold the Right Thumbstick and press Down, Up, Down, Down

INSTANT VICTORY

Click and hold the Right Thumbstick and press Up, Up, Up, Up

KILL ALL ALIENS

Click and hold the Right Thumbstick and press Left, Right, Left, Right

KILL ALL ALIENS CARRYING CORES

Click and hold the Right Thumbstick and press Up, Down, Down, Up

LEVEL SELECT

Click and hold the Right Thumbstick and press Up, Up, Down, Down, Left, Right, Left, Right

SELF-DESTRUCT (INSTANT DEFEAT)

Click and hold the Right Thumbstick and press Down, Down, Down, Down

TOGGLE TARGET RETICULE

Click and hold the Right Thumbstick and press Down, Up, Down, Up

UNLOCK ALL TOWER TYPES

Click and hold the Right Thumbstick and press Up, Down, Left, Right

DIRT 2

Win the given events to earn the following cars:

GET THIS CAR	BY WINNING THIS EVENT
Ford RS200 Evolution	Rally Cross World Tour
Toyota Stadium Truck	Landrush World Tour
Mitsubishi Pajero Dakar 1993	Raid World Tour
Dallenbach Special	Trailblazer World Tour
1995 Subaru Impreza WRX STi	Colin McRae Challenge
Colin McRae R4 [X Games]	X Games Europe
Mitsubishi Lancer Evolution X [X Games]	X Games Asia
Subaru Impreza WRX STi [X Games]	X Games America
Ford Escort MKII and MG Metro 6R4	All X Games events

DON KING PRESENTS: PRIZEFIGHTER

UNLOCK RICARDO MAYORGA

Select Enter Unlock Code from the Extras menu and enter potsemag.

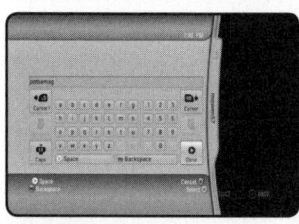 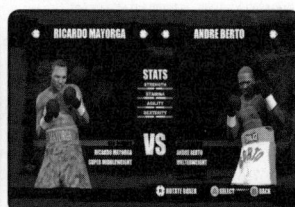

EXCLUSIVE BEST BUY FIGHT FOOTAGE

Select Enter Unlock Code from the Extras menu and enter 1bestbuybest. Select Watch Videos from the Extras menu to find video.

ERAGON

UNLIMITED FURY MODE

Pause the game, hold Left Bumper + Left Trigger + Right Bumper + Right Trigger and press Ⓧ, Ⓧ, Ⓑ, Ⓑ.

EVERY EXTEND EXTRA EXTREME

FINE ADJUSTMENT MENU

At the Start screen, press Left Bumper, Right Bumper, Left Bumper, Right Bumper, Left Bumper, Right Bumper, Left Bumper, Right Bumper.

FATAL FURY SPECIAL

CHEAT MENU

During a game, hold Start and push Ⓐ + Ⓧ + Ⓨ.

FIGHT NIGHT ROUND 3

ALL VENUES

Create a champ with a first name of NEWVIEW.

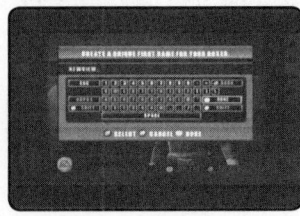 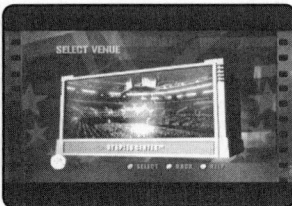

FLATOUT: ULTIMATE CARNAGE

MOB CAR IN SINGLE EVENTS

Select Enter Code from Extras and enter BIGTRUCK.

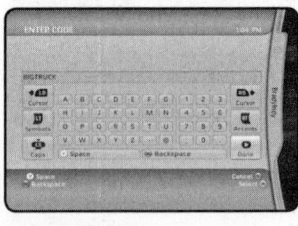 

PIMPSTER IN SINGLE EVENTS

Select Enter Code from Extras and enter RUTTO.

ROCKET IN SINGLE EVENTS

Select Enter Code from Extras and enter KALJAKOPPA.

FROGGER

BIG FROGGER

At the one/two player screen, press Up, Up, Down, Down, Left, Right, Left, Right, Ⓑ, Ⓐ.

FUEL

CAMO ARMY HELMET

Select Bonus Codes from the Options and enter 48992519.

ROAD ADDICT JACKET

Select Bonus Codes from the Options and enter 20061977.

SPEED ANGEL SHORTS

Select Bonus Codes from the Options and enter 91031985.

BUTTERFLY LIVERY FOR THE SLUDGERAY VEHICLE

Select Bonus Codes from the Options and enter 18021974.

LIGHTNING BOLT LIVERY FOR THE MUDHOG VEHICLE

Select Bonus Codes from the Options and enter 17121973.

WARRIOR VEHICLE

Select Bonus Codes from the Options and enter 18041851.

FULL AUTO

ALL TRACKS, VEHICLES, & WEAPONS

Create a new profile with the name magicman.

GAROU: MARK OF THE WOLVES

PLAY AS GRANT

Highlight Dong Hwan, hold Start, and press Up, Up, Down, Down, Up, Down. Press any button while still holding Start.

PLAY AS KAIN

Highlight Jae Hoon, hold Start, and press Down, Down, Up, Up, Down, Up. Press any button while still holding Start.

RANDOM CHARACTER SELECT

At the character select, hold Start and press a button.

G.I. JOE: THE RISE OF COBRA

CLASSIC DUKE

At the main menu, press Left, Up, ⊗, Up, Right, ⊙.

CLASSIC SCARLETT

At the main menu, press Right, Up, Down, Down, ⊙.

GRID

ALL DRIFT CARS

Select Bonus Codes from the Options. Then choose Enter Code and enter TUN58396.

ALL MUSCLE CARS

Select Bonus Codes from the Options. Then choose Enter Code and enter MUS59279.

BUCHBINDER EMOTIONAL ENGINEERING BMW 320SI

Select Bonus Codes from the Options. Then choose Enter Code and enter F93857372. You can use this in Race Day or in GRID World once you've started your own team.

EBAY

Select Bonus Codes from the Options. Then choose Enter Code and enter DAFJ55E01473M0. You can use this in Race Day or in GRID World once you've started your own team.

GAMESTATION BMW 320SI

Select Bonus Codes from the Options. Then choose Enter Code and enter G29782655. You can use this in Race Day or in GRID World once you've started your own team.

MICROMANIA PAGANI ZONDA R

Select Bonus Codes from the Options. Then choose Enter Code and enter M38572343. You can use this in Race Day or in GRID World once you've started your own team.

PLAY.COM ASTON MARTIN DBR9

Select Bonus Codes from the Options. Then choose Enter Code and enter P47203845. You can use this in Race Day or in GRID World once you've started your own team.

IDOLMASTER: LIVE FOR YOU!

MAMI

At the character select, press R3 while on Ami.

SHORT-HAIRED MIKI

At the character select, press R3 while on Miki.

IRON MAN

CLASSIC ARMOR
Clear One Man Army vs. Mercs.

EXTREMIS ARMOR
Clear One Man Army vs. Maggia.

MARK II ARMOR
Clear One Man Army vs. Ten Rings.

HULKBUSTER ARMOR
Clear One Man Army vs. AIM-X. Can also be unlocked when clear game save data from Incredible Hulk is stored on the same console.

SILVER CENTURION ARMOR
Clear Mission 13: Showdown.

CLASSIC MARK I ARMOR
Clear One Man Army vs. AIM.

JUICED 2: HOT IMPORT NIGHTS

FRITO-LAY INFINITY G35 CAR
Select Cheats and Codes from the DNA Lab menu and enter MNCH.

HIDDEN CHALLENGE AND AN AUDI TT 1.8 QUATTRO
Select Cheats and Codes from the DNA Lab menu and enter YTHZ. Defeat the challenge to earn the Audi TT 1.8 Quattro.

HIDDEN CHALLENGE AND A BMW Z4
Select Cheats and Codes from the DNA Lab menu and enter GVDL. Defeat the challenge to earn the BMW Z4.

HIDDEN CHALLENGE AND A HOLDEN MONARO
Select Cheats and Codes from the DNA Lab menu and enter 🎮 SG. Defeat the challenge to earn the Holden Monaro.

HIDDEN CHALLENGE AND A HYUNDAI COUPE 2.7 V6
Select Cheats and Codes from the DNA Lab menu and enter BSLU. Defeat the challenge to earn the Hyundai Coupe 2.7 V6.

HIDDEN CHALLENGE AND AN INFINITY G35
Select Cheats and Codes from the DNA Lab menu and enter MRHC. Defeat the challenge to earn the Infinity G35.

HIDDEN CHALLENGE AND A KOENIGSEGG CCX
Select Cheats and Codes from the DNA Lab menu and enter KDTR. Defeat the challenge to earn the Koenigsegg CCX.

HIDDEN CHALLENGE AND A MITSUBISHI PROTOTYPE X
Select Cheats and Codes from the DNA Lab menu and enter DOPX. Defeat the challenge to earn the Mitsubishi Prototype X.

HIDDEN CHALLENGE AND A NISSAN 350Z
Select Cheats and Codes from the DNA Lab menu and enter PRGN. Defeat the challenge to earn the Nissan 350Z.

HIDDEN CHALLENGE AND A NISSAN SKYLINE R34 GT-R

Select Cheats and Codes from the DNA Lab menu and enter JW⊕. Defeat the challenge to earn the Nissan Skyline R34 GT-R.

HIDDEN CHALLENGE AND A SALEEN S7

Select Cheats and Codes from the DNA Lab menu and enter WIKF. Defeat the challenge to earn the Saleen S7.

HIDDEN CHALLENGE AND A SEAT LEON CUPRA R

Select Cheats and Codes from the DNA Lab menu and enter FAMQ. Defeat the challenge to earn the Seat Leon Cupra R.

KUNG FU PANDA

INFINITE CHI

Select Cheats from the Extra menu and press Down, Right, Left, Up, Down.

INVINCIBILITY

Select Cheats from the Extra menu and press Down, Down, Right, Up, Left.

FULL UPGRADES

Select Cheats from the Extra menu and press Left, Right, Down, Left, Up.

4X DAMAGE MULTIPLIER

Select Cheats from the Extra menu and press Up, Down, Up, Right, Left.

ALL MULTIPLAYER CHARACTERS

Select Cheats from the Extra menu and press Left, Down, Left, Right, Down.

DRAGON WARRIOR OUTFIT IN MULTIPLAYER

Select Cheats from the Extra menu and press Left, Down, Right, Left, Up.

ALL OUTFITS

Select Cheats from the Extra menu and press Right, Left, Down, Up, Right.

THE LEGEND OF SPYRO: DAWN OF THE DRAGON

UNLIMITED LIFE

Pause the game, hold Left Bumper and press Right, Right, Down, Down, Left with the Left Control Stick.

UNLIMITED MANA

Pause the game, hold Right Bumper and press Up, Right, Up, Left, Down with the Left Control Stick.

MAXIMUM XP

Pause the game, hold Right Bumper and press Up, Left, Left, Down, Up with the Left Control Stick.

ALL ELEMENTAL UPGRADES

Pause the game, hold Left Bumper and press Left, Up, Down, Up, Right with the Left Control Stick.

BATCAVE CODES

Using the computer in the Batcave, select Enter Code and enter the following codes.

CHARACTERS

CHARACTER	CODE	CHARACTER	CODE
Alfred	ZAQ637	Penguin Henchman	BJH782
Batgirl	JKR331	Penguin Minion	KJP748
Bruce Wayne	BDJ327	Poison Ivy Goon	GTB899
Catwoman (Classic)	M1AAWW	Police Marksman	HKG984
Clown Goon	HJK327	Police Officer	JRY983
Commissioner Gordon	DDP967	Riddler Goon	CRY928
Fishmonger	HGY748	Riddler Henchman	XEU824
Freeze Girl	XVK541	S.W.A.T.	HTF114
Joker Goon	UTF782	Sailor	NAV592
Joker Henchman	YUN924	Scientist	JFL786
Mad Hatter	JCA283	Security Guard	PLB946
Man-Bat	NYU942	The Joker (Tropical)	CCB199
Military Policeman	MKL382	Yeti	NJL412
Nightwing	MVY759	Zoo Sweeper	DWR243
Penguin Goon	NKA238		

VEHICLES

VEHICLE	CODE	VEHICLE	CODE
Bat-Tank	KNTT4B	Mr. Freeze's Kart	BCT229
Bruce Wayne's Private Jet	LEA664	Penguin Goon Submarine	BTN248
Catwoman's Motorcycle	HPL826	Police Bike	LJP234
Garbage Truck	DUS483	Police Boat	PLC999
Goon Helicopter	GCH328	Police Car	KJL832
Harbor Helicopter	CHP735	Police Helicopter	CWR732
Harley Quinn's Hammer Truck	RDT637	Police Van	MAC788
Mad Hatter's Glider	HS000W	Police Watercraft	VJD328
Mad Hatter's Steamboat	M4DM4N	Riddler's Jet	HAHAHA
Mr. Freeze's Iceberg	ICYICE	Robin's Submarine	TTF453
The Joker's Van	JUK657	Two-Face's Armored Truck	EFE933

CHEATS

CHEAT	CODE	CHEAT	CODE
Always Score Multiply	9LRGNB	More Batarang Targets	XWP645
Fast Batarangs	JRBDCB	Piece Detector	KHJ554
Fast Walk	ZOLM6N	Power Brick Detector	MMN786
Flame Batarang	D8NYWH	Regenerate Hearts	HJH7HJ
Freeze Batarang	XPN4NG	Score x2	N4NR3E
Extra Hearts	ML3KHP	Score x4	CX9MAT
Fast Build	EVG26J	Score x6	MLVNF2
Immune to Freeze	JXUDY6	Score x8	WCCDB9
Invincibility	WYD5CP	Score x10	18HW07
Minikit Detector	ZXGH9J		

LEGO INDIANA JONES: THE ORIGINAL ADVENTURES

CHARACTERS

Approach the blackboard in the Classsroom and enter the following codes.

CHARACTER	CODE	CHARACTER	CODE
Bandit	12N68W	Fedora	V75YSP
Bandit Swordsman	1MK4RT	First Mate	0GIN24
Barranca	04EM94	Grail Knight	NE6THI
Bazooka Trooper (Crusade)	MK83R7	Hovitos Tribesman	H0V1SS
Bazooka Trooper (Raiders)	S93Y5R	Indiana Jones (Desert Disguise)	4J8S4M
Belloq	CHN3YU	Indiana Jones (Officer)	VJ850S
Belloq (Jungle)	TDR197	Jungle Guide	24PF34
Belloq (Robes)	VEO29L	Kao Kan	WMO46L
British Commander	B73EUA	Kazim	NRH23J
British Officer	VJ5TI9	Kazim (Desert)	3M29TJ
British Soldier	DJ5I2W	Lao Che	2NK479
Captain Katanga	VJ3TT3	Maharajah	NFK5N2
Chatter Lal	ENW936	Major Toht	13NS01
Chatter Lal (Thuggee)	CNH4RY	Masked Bandit	N48SF0
Chen	3NK48T	Mola Ram	FJUR31
Colonel Dietrich	2K9RKS	Monkey Man	3RF6YJ
Colonel Vogel	8EAL4H	Pankot Assassin	2NKT72
Dancing Girl	C7EJ21	Pankot Guard	VN28RH
Donovan	3NFTU8	Sherpa Brawler	VJ37WJ
Elsa (Desert)	JSNRT9	Sherpa Gunner	ND762W
Elsa (Officer)	VMJ5US	Slave Child	0E3ENW
Enemy Boxer	8246RB	Thuggee	VM683E
Enemy Butler	VJ48W3	Thuggee Acolyte	T2R3F9
Enemy Guard	VJ7R51	Thuggee Slave Driver	VBS7GW
Enemy Guard (Mountains)	YR47WM	Village Dignitary	KD48TN
Enemy Officer	572E61	Village Elder	4682E1
Enemy Officer (Desert)	2MK450	Willie (Dinner Suit)	VK93R7
Enemy Pilot	B84ELP	Willie (Pajamas)	MEN41P
Enemy Radio Operator	1MF94R	Wu Han	3NSLT8
Enemy Soldier (Desert)	4NSU7Q		

EXTRAS

Approach the blackboard in the Classsroom and enter the following codes. Some cheats need to be enabled by selecting Extras from the pause menu.

CHEAT	CODE	CHEAT	CODE
Artifact Detector	VIKED7	Regenerate Hearts	MDLP69
Beep Beep	VNF59Q	Secret Characters	3X44AA
Character Treasure	VIES2R	Silhouettes	3HE85H
Disarm Enemies	VKRNS9	Super Scream	VN3R7S
Disguises	4ID1N6	Super Slap	OP1TA5
Fast Build	V83SLO	Treasure Magnet	H86LA2
Fast Dig	378RS6	Treasure x10	VI3PS8
Fast Fix	FJ59WS	Treasure x2	VM4TS9
Fertilizer	B1GW1F	Treasure x4	VLWEN3
Ice Rink	33GM7J	Treasure x6	V84RYS
Parcel Detector	VUT673	Treasure x8	A72E1M
Poo Treasure	WWQ1SA		

LEGO STAR WARS II: THE ORIGINAL TRILOGY

BEACH TROOPER

At Mos Eisley Canteena, select Enter Code and enter UCK868. You still need to select
Characters and purchase this character for 20,000 studs.

BEN KENOBI (GHOST)

At Mos Eisley Canteena, select Enter Code and enter BEN917. You still need to select
Characters and purchase this character for 1,100,000 studs.

BESPIN GUARD

At Mos Eisley Canteena, select Enter Code and enter VHY832. You still need to select
Characters and purchase this character for 15,000 studs.

BIB FORTUNA

At Mos Eisley Canteena, select Enter Code and enter WTY721. You still need to select
Characters and purchase this character for 16,000 studs.

BOBA FETT

At Mos Eisley Canteena, select Enter Code and enter HLP221. You still need to select
Characters and purchase this character for 175,000 studs.

DEATH STAR TROOPER

At Mos Eisley Canteena, select Enter Code and enter BNC332. You still need to select
Characters and purchase this character for 19,000 studs.

EWOK

At Mos Eisley Canteena, select Enter Code and enter TTT289. You still need to select Characters
and purchase this character for 34,000 studs.

GAMORREAN GUARD

At Mos Eisley Canteena, select Enter Code and enter YZF999. You still need to select
Characters and purchase this character for 40,000 studs.

GONK DROID

At Mos Eisley Canteena, select Enter Code and enter NFX582. You still need to select
Characters and purchase this character for 1,550 studs.

GRAND MOFF TARKIN

At Mos Eisley Canteena, select Enter Code and enter SMG219. You still need to select
Characters and purchase this character for 38,000 studs.

GREEDO

At Mos Eisley Canteena, select Enter Code and enter NAH118. You still need to select
Characters and purchase this character for 60,000 studs.

HAN SOLO (HOOD)

At Mos Eisley Canteena, select Enter Code and enter YWM840. You still need to select
Characters and purchase this character for 20,000 studs.

IG-88

At Mos Eisley Canteena, select Enter Code and enter NXL973. You still need to select
Characters and purchase this character for 30,000 studs.

IMPERIAL GUARD

At Mos Eisley Canteena, select Enter Code and enter MMM111. You still need to select
Characters and purchase this character for 45,000 studs.

IMPERIAL OFFICER

At Mos Eisley Canteena, select Enter Code and enter BBV889. You still need to select Characters and purchase this character for 28,000 studs.

IMPERIAL SHUTTLE PILOT

At Mos Eisley Canteena, select Enter Code and enter VAP664. You still need to select Characters and purchase this character for 29,000 studs.

IMPERIAL SPY

At Mos Eisley Canteena, select Enter Code and enter CVT125. You still need to select Characters and purchase this character for 13,500 studs.

JAWA

At Mos Eisley Canteena, select Enter Code and enter JAW499. You still need to select Characters and purchase this character for 24,000 studs.

LOBOT

At Mos Eisley Canteena, select Enter Code and enter UUB319. You still need to select Characters and purchase this character for 11,000 studs.

PALACE GUARD

At Mos Eisley Canteena, select Enter Code and enter SGE549. You still need to select Characters and purchase this character for 14,000 studs.

REBEL PILOT

At Mos Eisley Canteena, select Enter Code and enter CYG336. You still need to select Characters and purchase this character for 15,000 studs.

REBEL TROOPER (HOTH)

At Mos Eisley Canteena, select Enter Code and enter EKU849. You still need to select Characters and purchase this character for 16,000 studs.

SANDTROOPER

At Mos Eisley Canteena, select Enter Code and enter YDV451. You still need to select Characters and purchase this character for 14,000 studs.

SKIFF GUARD

At Mos Eisley Canteena, select Enter Code and enter GBU888. You still need to select Characters and purchase this character for 12,000 studs.

SNOWTROOPER

At Mos Eisley Canteena, select Enter Code and enter NYU989. You still need to select Characters and purchase this character for 16,000 studs.

STROMTROOPER

At Mos Eisley Canteena, select Enter Code and enter PTR345. You still need to select Characters and purchase this character for 10,000 studs.

THE EMPEROR

At Mos Eisley Canteena, select Enter Code and enter HHY382. You still need to select Characters and purchase this character for 275,000 studs.

TIE FIGHTER

At Mos Eisley Canteena, select Enter Code and enter HDY739. You still need to select Characters and purchase this character for 60,000 studs.

TIE FIGHTER PILOT

At Mos Eisley Canteena, select Enter Code and enter NNZ316. You still need to select Characters and purchase this character for 21,000 studs.

TIE INTERCEPTOR

At Mos Eisley Canteena, select Enter Code and enter QYA828. You still need to select Characters and purchase this character for 40,000 studs.

TUSKEN RAIDER

At Mos Eisley Canteena, select Enter Code and enter PEJ821. You still need to select Characters and purchase this character for 23,000 studs.

UGNAUGHT

At Mos Eisley Canteena, select Enter Code and enter UGN694. You still need to select Characters and purchase this character for 36,000 studs.

LEGO STAR WARS: THE COMPLETE SAGA

The following still need to be purchase after entering the codes.

CHARACTERS

ADMIRAL ACKBAR

At the bar in Mos Eisley Cantina, select Enter Code and enter ACK646.

BATTLE DROID (COMMANDER)

At the bar in Mos Eisley Cantina, select Enter Code and enter KPF958.

BOBA FETT (BOY)

At the bar in Mos Eisley Cantina, select Enter Code and enter GGF539.

BOSS NASS

At the bar in Mos Eisley Cantina, select Enter Code and enter HHY697.

CAPTAIN TARPALS

At the bar in Mos Eisley Cantina, select Enter Code and enter QRN714.

COUNT DOOKU

At the bar in Mos Eisley Cantina, select Enter Code and enter DDD748.

DARTH MAUL

At the bar in Mos Eisley Cantina, select Enter Code and enter EUK421.

EWOK

At the bar in Mos Eisley Cantina, select Enter Code and enter EWK785.

GENERAL GRIEVOUS

At the bar in Mos Eisley Cantina, select Enter Code and enter PMN576.

GREEDO

At the bar in Mos Eisley Cantina, select Enter Code and enter ZZR636.

IG-88

At the bar in Mos Eisley Cantina, select Enter Code and enter GIJ989.

IMPERIAL GUARD

At the bar in Mos Eisley Cantina, select Enter Code and enter GUA850.

JANGO FETT

At the bar in Mos Eisley Cantina, select Enter Code and enter KLJ897.

KI-ADI MUNDI

At the bar in Mos Eisley Cantina, select Enter Code and enter MUN486.

LUMINARA

At the bar in Mos Eisley Cantina, select Enter Code and enter LUM521.

PADMÉ

At the bar in Mos Eisley Cantina, select Enter Code and enter VBJ322.

R2-Q5

At the bar in Mos Eisley Cantina, select Enter Code and enter EVILR2.

STORMTROOPER

At the bar in Mos Eisley Cantina, select Enter Code and enter NBN431.

TAUN WE

At the bar in Mos Eisley Cantina, select Enter Code and enter PRX482.

VULTURE DROID

At the bar in Mos Eisley Cantina, select Enter Code and enter BDC866.

WATTO

At the bar in Mos Eisley Cantina, select Enter Code and enter PLL967.

ZAM WESELL

At the bar in Mos Eisley Cantina, select Enter Code and enter 584HJF.

SKILLS

DISGUISE

At the bar in Mos Eisley Cantina, select Enter Code and enter BRJ437.

FORCE GRAPPLE LEAP

At the bar in Mos Eisley Cantina, select Enter Code and enter CLZ738.

VEHICLES

DROID TRIFIGHTER

At the bar in Mos Eisley Cantina, select Enter Code and enter AAB123.

IMPERIAL SHUTTLE

At the bar in Mos Eisley Cantina, select Enter Code and enter HUT845.

TIE INTERCEPTOR

At the bar in Mos Eisley Cantina, select Enter Code and enter INT729.

TIE FIGHTER

At the bar in Mos Eisley Cantina, select Enter Code and enter DBH897.

ZAM'S AIRSPEEDER

At the bar in Mos Eisley Cantina, select Enter Code and enter UUU875.

LOONEY TUNES: ACME ARSENAL

UNLIMITED AMMO

At the cheat menu, press Down, Left, Up, Right, Down, Left, Up, Right, Down.

104

LOST PLANET: EXTREME CONDITION

The following codes are for Single Player Mode on Easy Difficulty only.

500 THERMAL ENERGY

Pause the game and press Up, Up, Down, Down, Left, Right, Left, Right, ⊗, ⓨ, Right Bumper + Left Bumper.

INFINITE AMMUNITION

Pause the game and press Right Trigger, Right Bumper, ⓨ, ⊗, Right, Down, Left, Left Bumper, Left Trigger, Right Trigger, Right Bumper, ⓨ, ⊗, Right, Down, Left, Left Bumper, Left Trigger, Right Trigger, Left Trigger, Left Bumper, Right Bumper, ⓨ, Left, Down, ⊗, Right Bumper + Left Bumper.

INFINITE HEALTH

Pause the game and press Down (x3), Up, ⓨ, Up, ⓨ, Up, ⓨ, Up(x3), Down, ⊗, Down, ⊗, Down, ⊗, Left, ⓨ, Right, ⊗, –Left, ⓨ, Right, ⊗, Right Bumper + Left Bumper.

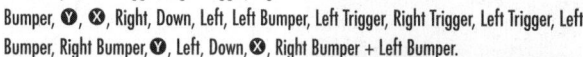

CHANGE CAMERA ANGLE IN CUT SCENES

During a cut scene, press Ⓑ, ⓐ, ⓧ, ⓨ, Ⓑ, ⓐ, ⓧ, ⓨ, Ⓑ, ⓐ, ⓧ, ⓨ.

MAJOR LEAGUE BASEBALL 2K6

UNLOCK EVERYTHING

Select Enter Cheat Code from the My 2K6 menu and enter Derek Jeter.

TOPPS 2K STARS

Select Enter Cheat Code from the My 2K6 menu and enter Dream Team.

SUPER WALL CLIMB

Select Enter Cheat Code from the My 2K6 menu and enter Last Chance. Enable the cheats by selecting My Cheats or selecting Cheat Codes from the in-game Options screen.

SUPER PITCHES

Select Enter Cheat Code from the My 2K6 menu and enter Unhittable. Enable the cheats by selecting My Cheats or selecting Cheat Codes from the in-game Options screen.

ROCKET ARMS

Select Enter Cheat Code from the My 2K6 menu and enter Gotcha. Enable the cheats by selecting My Cheats or selecting Cheat Codes from the in-game Options screen.

BOUNCY BALL

Select Enter Cheat Code from the My 2K6 menu and enter Crazy Hops. Enable the cheats by selecting My Cheats or selecting Cheat Codes from the in-game Options.

MAJOR LEAGUE BASEBALL 2K7

MICKEY MANTLE ON THE FREE AGENTS LIST

Select Enter Cheat Code from the My 2K7 menu and enter themick.

ALL CHEATS

Select Enter Cheat Code from the My 2K7 menu and enter Black Sox.

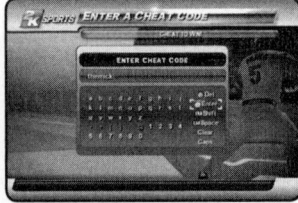 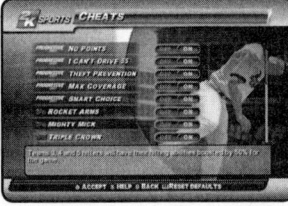

ALL EXTRAS

Select Enter Cheat Code from the My 2K7 menu and enter Game On.

UNLOCK EVERYTHING

Select Enter Cheat Code from the My 2K7 menu and enter Derek Jeter. This does not unlock the Topps cheats.

MIGHTY MICK CHEAT

Select Enter Cheat Code from the My 2K7 menu and enter mightymick.

TRIPLE CROWN CHEAT

Select Enter Cheat Code from the My 2K7 menu and enter triplecrown.

PINCH HIT MICK CHEAT

Select Enter Cheat Code from the My 2K7 menu and enter phmantle.

BIG BLAST CHEAT

Select Enter Cheat Code from the My 2K7 menu Rand enter m4murder.

MARVEL ULTIMATE ALLIANCE

UNLOCK ALL SKINS

At the Team menu, press Up, Down, Left, Right, Left, Right, Start.

UNLOCKS ALL HERO POWERS
At the Team menu, press Left, Right, Up, Down, Up, Down, Start.

ALL HEROES TO LEVEL 99
At the Team menu, press Up, Left, Up, Left, Down, Right, Down, Right, Start.

UNLOCK ALL HEROES
At the Team menu, press Up, Up, Down, Down, Left, Left, Left, Start.

UNLOCK DAREDEVIL
At the Team menu, press Left, Left, Right, Right, Up, Down, Up, Down, Start.

UNLOCK SILVER SURFER
At the Team menu, press Down, Left, Left, Up, Right, Up, Down, Left, Start.

GOD MODE
During gameplay, press Up, Down, Up, Down, Up, Left, Down, Right, Start.

TOUCH OF DEATH
During gameplay, press Left, Right, Down, Down, Right, Left, Start.

SUPER SPEED
During gameplay, press Up, Left, Up, Right, Down, Right, Start.

FILL MOMENTUM
During gameplay, press Left, Right, Right, Left, Up, Down, Down, Up, Start.

UNLOCK ALL COMICS
At the Review menu, press Left, Right, Right, Left, Up, Up, Right, Start.

UNLOCK ALL CONCEPT ART
At the Review menu, press Down, Down, Down, Right, Right, Left, Down, Start.

UNLOCK ALL CINEMATICS
At the Review menu, press Up, Left, Left, Up, Right, Right, Up, Start.

UNLOCK ALL LOAD SCREENS
At the Review menu, press Up, Down, Right, Left, Up, Up Down, Start.

UNLOCK ALL COURSES
At the Comic Missions menu, press Up, Right, Left, Down, Up, Right, Left, Down, Start.

MARVEL: ULTIMATE ALLIANCE 2

These codes will disable the ability to save.

GOD MODE
During a game, press Up, Down, Up, Down, Up, Left, Down, Right, Start.

UNLIMITED FUSION
During a game, press Right, Right, Up, Down, Up, Up, Left, Start.

UNLOCK ALL POWERS
During a game, press Left, Right, Up, Down, Up, Down, Start.

UNLOCK ALL HEROES
During a game, press Up, Up, Down, Down, Left, Left, Start.

UNLOCK ALL SKINS
During a game, press Up, Down, Left, Right, Left, Right, Start.

UNLOCK JEAN GREY
During a game, press Left, Left, Right, Right, Up, Down, Up, Down, Start.

UNLOCK HULK

During a game, press Down, Left, Left, Up, Right, Up, Down, Left, Start.

UNLOCK THOR

During a game, press Up, Right, Right, Down, Right, Down, Left, Right, Start.

UNLOCK ALL AUDIO LOGS

At the main menu, press Left, Right, Right, Left, Up, Up, Right, Start.

UNLOCK ALL DOSSIERS

At the main menu, press Down, Down, Down, Right, Right, Left, Down, Start.

UNLOCK ALL MOVIES

At the main menu, press Up, Left, Left, Up, Right, Right, Up, Start.

MONSTER MADNESS: BATTLE FOR SUBURBIA

Pause the game and press Up, Up, Down, Down, Left, Right, Left, Right, **B**, **A**. This brings up a screen where you can enter the following cheats. With the use of some cheats profile saving, level progression, and Xbox Live Achievements are disabled until you return to the Main menu.

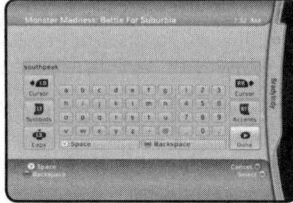

EFFECT	CHEAT
Animal Sounds	patrickdugan
Disable Tracking Cameras	ihatefunkycameras
Faster Music	upthejoltcola
First Person	morgythemole

EFFECT	CHEAT
Infinite Secondary Items	stevebrooks
Objects Move Away from Player	southpeak
Remove Film Grain	reverb

MOTOGP 07

ALL CHALLENGES

At the main menu, press Right, Up, **B**, **A**, **B**, **A**, Left, Down, **Y**.

ALL CHAMPIONSHIPS

At the main menu, press Right, Up, **B**, **Y**, Right, Up, **B**, **Y**, Right, Up, **B**, **Y**.

ALL LIVERIES

At the main menu, press Right, **A**, Left, Left, **Y**, Left, **A**, Down, **Y**.

ALL RIDERS

At the main menu, press Right, Up, **B**, **B**, **A**, Down, Up, **B**, Down, Up, **B**.

ALL TRACKS

At the main menu, press Left, **A**, Right, Down, **Y**, **B**, **A**, **B**, **Y**.

MX VS. ATV UNTAMED

ALL RIDING GEAR
Select Cheat Codes from the Options and enter crazylikea.

ALL HANDLEBARS
Select Cheat Codes from the Options and enter nohands.

27 GRAPHICS
Select Cheat Codes from the Options and enter STICKE⊛.

NARUTO: THE BROKEN BOND

NINE TAILS NARUTO
At the Character Select press ⊗, ⊗, ⓨ, ⓨ, ⊗, ⓨ, ⊗, ⓨ, ⊗, ⊗.

NASCAR 08

ALL CHASE MODE CARS
Select Cheat Codes from the Options menu and enter checkered flag.

EA SPORTS CAR
Select Cheat Codes from the Options menu and enter ea sports car.

FANTASY DRIVERS
Select Cheat Codes from the Options menu and enter race the pack.

WALMART CAR AND TRACK
Select Cheat Codes from the Options menu and enter walmart everyday.

NASCAR 09

ALL FANTASY DRIVERS
Select EA Extras from My Nascar, choose Cheat Codes and enter CHECKERED FLAG.

WALMART TRACK AND THE WALMART CAR
Select EA Extras from My Nascar, choose Cheat Codes and enter Walmart Everyday.

NBA 2K7

MAX DURABILITY
Select Codes from the Features menu and enter ironman.

UNLIMITED STAMINA
Select Codes from the Features menu and enter norest.

+10 DEFFENSIVE AWARENESS
Select Codes from the Features menu and enter getstops.

+10 OFFENSIVE AWARENESS
Select Codes from the Features menu and enter inthezone.

TOPPS 2K SPORTS ALL-STARS
Select Codes from the Features menu and enter topps2ksports.

ABA BALL
Select Codes from the Features menu and enter payrespect.

NBA 2K8

2KSPORTS TEAM

Select Codes from the Features menu and enter 2ksports.

VISUAL CONCEPTS TEAM

Select Codes from the Features menu and enter Vcteam.

ABA BALL

Select Codes from the Features menu and enter Payrespect.

NBA 2K9

2K SPORTS TEAM

Select Codes from the Features menu and enter 2ksports.

NBA 2K TEAM

 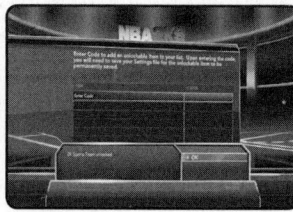

Select Codes from the Features menu and enter nba2k.

2K CHINA TEAM

Select Codes from the Features menu and enter 2kchina.

SUPERSTARS

Select Codes from the Features menu and enter llmohffaae.

VC TEAM

Select Codes from the Features menu and enter vcteam.

ABA BALL

Select Codes from the Features menu and enter payrespect.

2009 ALL-STAR UNIFORMS

Select Codes from the Features menu and enter llaveyfonus.

NBA 2K10

ABA BALL

Select Codes from Options and enter payrespect.

2K CHINA TEAM

Select Codes from Options and enter 2kchina.

NBA 2K TEAM

Select Codes from Options and enter nba2k.

2K SPORTS TEAM

Select Codes from Options and enter 2ksports.

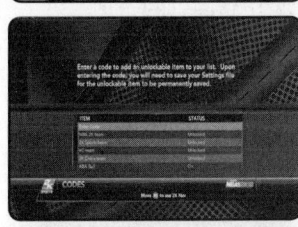

VISUAL CONCEPTS TEAM

Select Codes from Options and enter vcteam.

NBA LIVE 07

ADIDAS ARTILLERY II BLACK AND THE RBK ANSWER 9 VIDEO

Select NBA Codes from My NBA Live and enter 99B6356HAN.

ADIDAS ARTILLERY II

Select NBA Codes and enter NTGNFUE87H.

ADIDAS BTB LOW AND THE MESSAGE FROM ALLEN IVERSON VIDEO

Select NBA Codes and enter 7FB3KS9JQ0.

ADIDAS C-BILLUPS

Select NBA Codes and enter BV6877HB9N.

ADIDAS C-BILLUPS BLACK

Select NBA Codes and enter 85NVLDMWS5.

ADIDAS CAMPUS LT

Select NBA Codes and enter CLT2983NC8.

ADIDAS CRAZY 8

Select NBA Codes and enter CC98KKL814.

ADIDAS EQUIPMENT BBALL
Select NBA Codes and enter 220IUJKMDR.

ADIDAS GARNETT BOUNCE
Select NBA Codes and enter HYIOUHCAAN.

ADIDAS GARNETT BOUNCE BLACK
Select NBA Codes and enter KDZ2MQL17W.

ADIDAS GIL-ZERO
Select NBA Codes and enter 23DN1PPOG4.

ADIDAS GIL-ZERO BLACK
Select NBA Codes and enter QQQ3JCUYQ7.

ADIDAS GIL-ZERO MID
Select NBA Codes and enter 1GSJC8JWRL.

ADIDAS GIL-ZERO MID BLACK
Select NBA Codes and enter 369V6RVU3G.

ADIDAS STEALTH
Select NBA Codes and enter FE454DFJCC.

ADIDAS T-MAC 6
Select NBA Codes and enter MCJK843NNC.

ADIDAS T-MAC 6 WHITE
Select NBA Codes and enter 84GF7EJG8V.

CHARLOTTE BOBCATS 2006-2007 ALTERNATE JERSEY
Select NBA Codes and enter WEDX671H7S.

UTAH JAZZ 2006-2007 ALTERNATE JERSEY
Select NBA Codes and enter VCBI89FK83.

NEW JERSEY NETS 2006-2007 ALTERNATE JERSEY
Select NBA Codes and enter D4SAA98U5H.

WASHINGTON WIZARDS 2006-2007 ALTERNATE JERSEY
Select NBA Codes and enter QV93NLKXQC.

EASTERN ALL-STARS 2006-2007 AWAY JERSEY
Select NBA Codes and enter WOCNW4KL7L.

EASTERN ALL-STARS 2006-2007 HOME JERSEY
Select NBA Codes and enter 5654ND43N6.

WESTERN ALL-STARS 2006-2007 AWAY JERSEY
Select NBA Codes and enter XX93BVL20U.

WESTERN ALL-STARS 2006-2007 HOME JERSEY
Select NBA Codes and enter 993NSKL199.

NBA LIVE 09

SUPER DUNKS MODE
Use the Sprite vending machine in the practice area and enter spriteslam.

NBA STREET HOMECOURT

ALL TEAMS
At the Main menu, hold Right Bumper + Left Bumper and press Left, Right, Left, Right.

ALL COURTS
At the Main menu, hold Right Bumper + Left Bumper and press Up, Right, Down, Left.

BLACK/RED BALL
At the Main menu, hold Right Bumper + Left Bumper and press Up, Down, Left, Right.

NCAA FOOTBALL 07

#16 BAYLOR
Select Pennant Collection from My NCAA. Press Select and enter Sic Em.

#16 NIKE SPEED TD
Select Pennant Collection from My NCAA. Press Select and enter Light Speed.

#63 ILLINOIS
Select Pennant Collection from My NCAA. Press Select and enter Oskee Wow.

#160 TEXAS TECH
Select Pennant Collection from My NCAA. Press Select and enter Fight.

#200 FIRST AND FIFTEEN
Select Pennant Collection from My NCAA. Press Select and enter Thanks.

#201 BLINK
Select Pennant Collection from My NCAA. Press Select and enter For.

#202 BOING
Select Pennant Collection from My NCAA. Press Select and enter Registering.

#204 BUTTER FINGERS
Select Pennant Collection from My NCAA. Press Select and enter With EA.

#205 CROSSED THE LINE
Select Pennant Collection from My NCAA. Press Select and enter Tiburon.

#206 CUFFED
Select Pennant Collection from My NCAA. Press Select and enter EA Sports.

#207 EXTRA CREDIT
Select Pennant Collection from My NCAA. Press Select and enter Touchdown.

#208 HELIUM
Select Pennant Collection from My NCAA. Press Select and enter In The Zone.

#209 HURRICANE
Select Pennant Collection from My NCAA. Press Select and enter Turnover.

#210 INSTANT FREPLAY
Select Pennant Collection from My NCAA. Press Select and enter Impact.

#211 JUMBALAYA
Select Pennant Collection from My NCAA. Press Select and enter Heisman.

#212 MOLASSES
Select Pennant Collection from My NCAA. Press Select and enter Game Time.

#213 NIKE FREE
Select Pennant Collection from My NCAA. Press Select and enter Break Free.

#214 NIKE MAGNIGRIP
Select Pennant Collection from My NCAA. Press Select and enter Hand Picked.

#215 NIKE PRO
Select Pennant Collection from My NCAA. Press Select and enter No Sweat.

#219 QB DUD
Select Pennant Collection from My NCAA. Press Select and enter Elite 11.

#221 STEEL TOE
Select Pennant Collection from My NCAA. Press Select and enter Gridiron.

#222 STIFFED
Select Pennant Collection from My NCAA. Press Select and enter NCAA.

#223 SUPER DIVE
Select Pennant Collection from My NCAA. Press Select and enter Upset.

#224 TAKE YOUR TIME
Select Pennant Collection from My NCAA. Press Select and enter Football.

#225 THREAD & NEEDLE
Select Pennant Collection from My NCAA. Press Select and enter 06.

#226 TOUGH AS NAILS
Select Pennant Collection from My NCAA. Press Select and enter Offense.

#227 TRIP
Select Pennant Collection from My NCAA. Press Select and enter Defense.

#228 WHAT A HIT
Select Pennant Collection from My NCAA. Press Select and enter Blitz.

#229 KICKER HEX
Select Pennant Collection from My NCAA. Press Select and enter Sideline.

#273 2004 ALL-AMERICANS
Select Pennant Collection from My NCAA. Press Select and enter Fumble.

#274 ALL-ALABAMA
Select Pennant Collection from My NCAA. Press Select and enter Roll Tide.

#276 ALL-ARKANSAS
Select Pennant Collection from My NCAA. Press Select and enter Woopigsooie.

#277 ALL-AUBURN
Select Pennant Collection from My NCAA. Press Select and enter War Eagle.

#278 ALL-CLEMSON
Select Pennant Collection from My NCAA. Press Select and enter Death Valley.

#279 ALL-COLORADO
Select Pennant Collection from My NCAA. Press Select and enter Glory.

#280 ALL-FLORIDA
Select Pennant Collection from My NCAA. Press Select and enter Great To Be.

#281 ALL-FSU
Select Pennant Collection from My NCAA. Press Select and enter Uprising.

#282 ALL-GEORGIA
Select Pennant Collection from My NCAA. Press Select and enter Hunker Down.

#283 ALL-IOWA
Select Pennant Collection from My NCAA. Press Select and enter On Iowa.

#284 ALL-KANSAS STATE
Select Pennant Collection from My NCAA. Press Select and enter Victory.

#285 ALL-LSU
Select Pennant Collection from My NCAA. Press Select and enter Geaux Tigers.

#286 ALL-MIAMI
Select Pennant Collection from My NCAA. Press Select and enter Raising Cane.

#287 ALL-MICHIGAN
Select Pennant Collection from My NCAA. Press Select and enter Go Blue.

#288 ALL-MISSISSIPPI STATE
Select Pennant Collection from My NCAA. Press Select and enter Hail State.

#289 ALL-NEBRASKA
Select Pennant Collection from My NCAA. Press Select and enter Go Big Red.

#290 ALL-NORTH CAROLINA
Select Pennant Collection from My NCAA. Press Select and enter Rah Rah.

#291 ALL-NOTRE DAME
Select Pennant Collection from My NCAA. Press Select and enter Golden Domer.

#292 ALL-OHIO STATE
Select Pennant Collection from My NCAA. Press Select and enter Killer Nuts.

#293 ALL-OKLAHOMA
Select Pennant Collection from My NCAA. Press Select and enter Boomer.

#294 ALL-OKLAHOMA STATE
Select Pennant Collection from My NCAA. Press Select and enter Go Pokes.

#295 ALL-OREGON
Select Pennant Collection from My NCAA. Press Select and enter Quack Attack.

#296 ALL-PENN STATE
Select Pennant Collection from My NCAA. Press Select and enter We Are.

#297 ALL-PITTSBURGH
Select Pennant Collection from My NCAA. Press Select and enter Lets Go Pitt.

#298 ALL-PURDUE
Select Pennant Collection from My NCAA. Press Select and enter Boiler Up.

#299 ALL-SYRACUSE

Select Pennant Collection from My NCAA. Press Select and enter Orange Crush.

#300 ALL-TENNESSEE

Select Pennant Collection from My NCAA. Press Select and enter Big Orange.

#301 ALL-TEXAS

Select Pennant Collection from My NCAA. Press Select and enter Hook Em.

#302 ALL-TEXAS A&M

Select Pennant Collection from My NCAA. Press Select and enter Gig Em.

#303 ALL-UCLA

Select Pennant Collection from My NCAA. Press Select and enter MIGHTY.

#304 ALL-USC

Select Pennant Collection from My NCAA. Press Select and enter Fight On.

#305 ALL-VIRGINIA

Select Pennant Collection from My NCAA. Press Select and enter Wahoos.

#306 ALL-VIRGINIA TECH

Select Pennant Collection from My NCAA. Press Select and enter Tech Triumph.

#307 ALL-WASHINGTON

Select Pennant Collection from My NCAA. Press Select and enter Bow Down.

#308 ALL-WISCONSIN

Select Pennant Collection from My NCAA. Press Select and enter U Rah Rah.

#311 ARK MASCOT

Select Pennant Collection from My NCAA. Press Select and enter Bear Down.

#329 GT MASCOT

Select Pennant Collection from My NCAA. Press Select and enter RamblinWreck.

#333 ISU MASCOT

Select Pennant Collection from My NCAA. Press Select and enter Red And Gold.

#335 KU MASCOT

Select Pennant Collection from My NCAA. Press Select and enter Rock Chalk.

#341 MINN MASCOT

Select Pennant Collection from My NCAA. Press Select and enter Rah Rah Rah.

#344 MIZZOU MASCOT

Select Pennant Collection from My NCAA. Press Select and enter Mizzou Rah.

#346 MSU MASCOT

Select Pennant Collection from My NCAA. Press Select and enter Go Green.

#349 NCSU MASCOT

Select Pennant Collection from My NCAA. Press Select and enter Go Pack.

#352 NU MASCOT

Select Pennant Collection from My NCAA. Press Select and enter Go Cats.

#360 S CAR MASCOT

Select Pennant Collection from My NCAA. Press Select and enter Go Carolina.

#371 UK MASCOT

Select Pennant Collection from My NCAA. Press Select and enter On On UK.

#382 WAKE FOREST
Select Pennant Collection from My NCAA. Press Select and enter Go Deacs Go.

#385 WSU MASCOT
Select Pennant Collection from My NCAA. Press Select and enter All Hail.

#386 WVU MASCOT
Select Pennant Collection from My NCAA. Press Select and enter Hail WV.

NEED FOR SPEED CARBON

CASTROL CASH
At the Main menu, press Down, Up, Left, Down, Right, Up, ✖, Ⓑ. This will give you 10,000 extra cash.

INFINITE CREW CHARGE
At the Main menu, press Down, Up, Up, Right, Left, Left, Right, ✖.

INFINITE NITROUS
At the Main menu, press Left, Up, Left, Down, Left, Down, Right, ✖.

INFINITE SPEEDBREAKER
At the Main menu, press Down, Right, Right, Left, Right, Up, Down, ✖.

NEED FOR SPEED CARBON LOGO VINYLS
At the Main menu, press Right, Up, Down, Up, Down, Left, Right, ✖.

NEED FOR SPEED CARBON SPECIAL LOGO VINYLS
At the Main menu, press Up, Up, Down, Down, Down, Down, Up, ✖.

NEED FOR SPEED PROSTREET

$2,000
Select Career and then choose Code Entry. Enter 1MA9X99.

$4,000
Select Career and then choose Code Entry. Enter W2IOLLO1.

$8,000
Select Career and then choose Code Entry. Enter L1IS97A1.

$10,000
Select Career and then choose Code Entry. Enter 1MI9K7E1.

$10,000
Select Career and then choose Code Entry. Enter CASHMONEY.

$10,000
Select Career and then choose Code Entry. Enter REGGAME.

AUDI TT
Select Career and then choose Code Entry. Enter ITSABOUTYOU.

CHEVELLE SS
Select Career and then choose Code Entry. Enter HO ⊙ EPOWER.

COKE ZERO GOLF GTI
Select Career and then choose Code Entry. Enter COKEZERO.

DODGE VIPER

Select Career and then choose Code Entry. Enter WORLDSLONGESTLASTING.

MITSUBISHI LANCER EVOLUTION

Select Career and then choose Code Entry. Enter MITSUBISHIGOFAR.

UNLOCK ALL BONUSES

Select Career and then choose Code Entry. Enter UNLOCKALLTHINGS.

5 REPAIR MARKERS

Select Career and then choose Code Entry. Enter SAFETYNET.

ENERGIZER VINYL

Select Career and then choose Code Entry. Enter ENERGIZERLITHIUM.

CASTROL SYNTEC VINYL

Select Career and then choose Code Entry. Enter CASTRO ⬛ YNTEC. This also gives you $10,000.

NEED FOR SPEED UNDERCOVER

$10,000

Select Secret Codes from the Options menu and enter $EDSOC.

DIE-CAST BMW M3 E92

Select Secret Codes from the Options menu and enter)B7@B=.

DIE-CAST LEXUS IS F

Select Secret Codes from the Options menu and enter 0;5M2;.

NEEDFORSPEED.COM LOTUS ELISE

Select Secret Codes from the Options menu and enter -KJ3=E.

DIE-CAST NISSAN 240SX (S13)

Select Secret Codes from the Options menu and enter ?P:COL.

DIE-CAST PORSCHE 911 TURBO

Select Secret Codes from the Options menu and enter >8P:I;.

SHELBY TERLINGUA

Select Secret Codes from the Options menu and enter NeedForSpeedShelbyTerlingua.

DIE-CAST VOLKSWAGEN R32

Select Secret Codes from the Options menu and enter!2ODBJ:.

NHL 08

ALL RBK EDGE JERSEYS

At the ⬛ K Edge Code option, enter h3oyxpwksf8ibcgt.

NHL 2K8

2007-2008 NHL REEBOK EDGE JERSEYS

From the Features menu, select Unlock 2007-2008/Enter Password. Enter S6j83RMk01.

 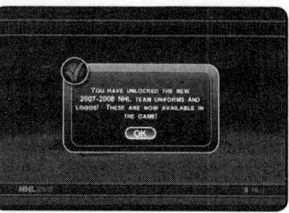

NHL 2K9

3RD JERSEYS

From the Features menu, enter R6y34bsH52 as a code.

NPPL CHAMPIONSHIP PAINTBALL 2009

TIPPMANN X-7 AK-47 SCENARIO PAINTBALL MARKER

Select Field Gear and press Up, Up, Right, Right, Down, Down, Left, Left.

PETER JACKSON'S KING KONG: THE OFFICIAL GAME OF THE MOVIE

At the Main menu hold Left Bumper + Right Bumper + Left Trigger + Right Trigger and press Down, Up, **Y**, **X**, Down, Down, **Y**, **Y**. Release the buttons to access the Cheat option. The Cheat option will also be available on the pause menu. You cannot record your scores using cheat codes.

GOD MODE

Select Cheat and enter 8wonder.

ALL CHAPTERS

Select Cheat and enter KKst0ry.

AMMO 999

Select Cheat and enter KK 999 mun.

MACHINE GUN

Select Cheat and enter KKcapone.

REVOLVER

Select Cheat and enter KKtigun.

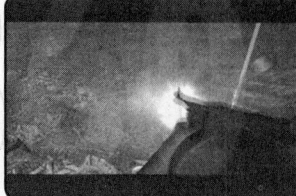

SNIPER RIFLE

Select Cheat and enter KKsn1per.

INFINITE SPEARS

Select Cheat and enter lance 1nf.

ONE-HIT KILLS

Select Cheat and enter GrosBras.

EXTRAS

Select Cheat and enter KKmuseum.

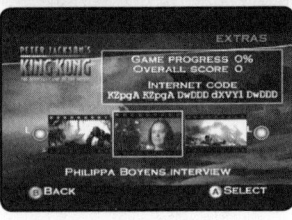

PRINCE OF PERSIA

SANDS OF TIME PRINCE/FARAH SKINS

Select Skin Manager from the Extras menu. Press Ⓨ and enter 52585854. This gives you the Sands of Time skin for the Prince and Farah from Sands of Time for the Princess. Access them from the Skin Manager

PRINCE ALTAIR IBN LA-AHAD SKIN

At the main menu, press Y for Exclusive Content. Create an Ubisoft account. Then select "Altair Skin for Prince" to unlock.

RATATOUILLE

UNLIMITED RUNNING

At the Cheat Code screen, enter SPEEDY.

ALL MULTIPLAYER AND SINGLE PLAYER MINI GAMES

At the Cheat Code screen, enter MATTELME.

ROCKSTAR GAMES PRESENTS TABLE TENNIS

Use of the following codes will disable achievements.

SWEATY CHARACTER VIEWER

After loading the map and before accepting the match, press Right Trigger, Up, Down, Left Trigger, Left, Right, Ⓨ, Ⓧ, Ⓧ, Ⓨ.

SMALL CROWD AUDIO

After loading the map and before accepting the match, press Down, Down, Down, Left Bumper, Left Trigger, Left Bumper, Left Trigger.

BIG BALL
After loading the map and before accepting the match, press Left, Right, Left, Right, Up, Up, Up, **⊗**.

COLORBLIND SPINDICATOR (ONLY IN NEWER PATCH)
After loading the map and before accepting the match, press Up, Down, **⊗**, **⊗**, **Ⓨ**, **Ⓨ**.

SILHOUETTE MODE
After loading the map and before accepting the match, press Up, Down, **Ⓨ**, **Ⓨ**, Left Bumper, Left Trigger, Right Trigger, Right Bumper.

BIG PADDLES CHEAT (ONLY IN NEWER PATCH)
After loading the map and before accepting the match, press Up, Left, Up, Right, Up, Down, Up, Up, **⊗**, **⊗**.

UNLOCK ALL
After loading the map and before accepting the match, press Up, Right, Down, Left, Left Bumper, Right, Up, Left, Down, Right Bumper.

VINTAGE AUDIO
After loading the map and before accepting the match, press Up, Up, Down, Down, Left, Right, Left, Right, Left Bumper, Right Bumper.

BIG CROWD AUDIO
After loading the map and before accepting the match, press Up, Up, Up, Right Bumper, Right Trigger, Right Bumper, Right Trigger.

OFFLINE GAMERTAGS
After loading the map and before accepting the match, press **⊗**, **Ⓨ**, **⊗**, **Ⓨ**, **⊗**, **Ⓨ**, Left Trigger, Right Trigger, Down, Down, Down.

SAMURAI SHODOWN 2

PLAY AS KUROKO IN 2-PLAYER
At the character select, press Up, Down, Left, Up, Down, Right + **⊗**.

SEGA SUPERSTARS TENNIS

UNLOCK CHARACTERS
Complete the following missions to unlock the corresponding character.

CHARACTER	MISSION TO COMPLETE
Alex Kidd	Mission 1 of Alex Kidd's World
Amy Rose	Mission 2 of Sonic the Hedgehog's World
Gilius	Mission 1 of Golden Axe's World
Gum	Mission 12 of Jet Grind Radio's World
Meemee	Mission 8 of Super Monkey Ball's World
Pudding	Mission 1 of Space Channel 5's World
Reala	Mission 2 of NiGHTs' World
Shadow The Hedgehog	Mission 14 of Sonic the Hedgehog's World

SHREK THE THIRD

10,000 GOLD COINS

At the gift shop, press Up, Up, Down, Up, Right, Left.

THE SIMPSONS GAME

After unlocking the following, the outfits can be changed at the downstairs closet in the Simpson's house. The Trophies can be viewed at different locations in the house: Bart's room, Lisa's room, Marge's room, and the garage.

BART'S OUTFITS AND TROPHIES (POSTER COLLECTION)

At the main menu, press Right, Left, ✗, ✗, Y, Right Thumb Stick.

HOMER'S OUTFITS AND TROPHIES (BEER BOTTLE COLLECTION)

At the main menu, press Left, Right, Y, Y, ✗, Left Thumb Stick.

LISA'S OUTFITS AND TROPHIES (DOLLS)

At the main menu, press ✗, Y, ✗, ✗, Y, Left Thumb Stick.

MARGE'S OUTFITS AND TROPHIES (HAIR PRODUCTS)

At the main menu, press Y, ✗, Y, Y, ✗, Right Thumb Stick.

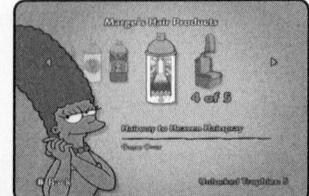 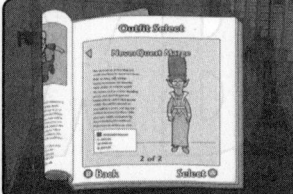

SKATE

EXCLUSIVE BEST BUY CLOTHES

At the Main Menu, press Up, Down, Left, Right, ❌, Right Bumper, ❓, Left Bumper. You can get the clothes at Reg's or Slappy's Skate Shop. Find it under Skate.

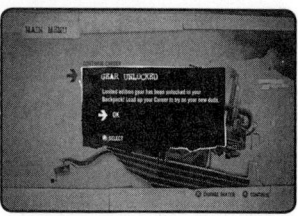

DEM BONES CHARACTER

Break each bone in your body at least 3 times.

SKATE 2

BIG BLACK

Select Enter Cheat from the Extras menu and enter letsdowork.

3D MODE

Select Enter Cheat from the Extras menu and enter strangeloops. Use glasses to view in 3D.

SPIDER-MAN: FRIEND OR FOE

NEW GREEN GOBLIN AS A SIDEKICK

While standing in the Helicarrier between levels, press Left, Down, Right, Right, Down, Left.

SANDMAN AS A SIDEKICK

While standing in the Helicarrier between levels, press Right, Right, Right, Up, Down, Left.

VENOM AS A SIDEKICK

While standing in the Helicarrier between levels, press Left, Left, Right, Up, Down, Down.

5000 TECH TOKENS

While standing in the Helicarrier between levels, press Up, Up, Down, Down, Left, Right.

STAR TREK: D-A-C

KOBAYASHI MARU CHEAT AND ACHIEVEMENT

Once a match begins, pause the game, and press Left Trigger, ❓, ❌, ❌, ❓, Right Trigger. This increases your rate of fire and regeneration. This also gives you the Kobayashi Maru achievement.

STAR WARS: THE FORCE UNLEASHED

CHEAT CODES

Pause the game and select Input Code. Here you can enter the following codes. Activating any of the following cheat codes will disable some unlockables, and you will be unable to save your progress.

CHEAT	CODE	CHEAT	CODE
All Force Powers at Max Power	KATARN	All Saber Crystals	HURRIKANE
All Force Push Ranks	EXARKUN	All Talents	JOCASTA
All Saber Throw Ranks	ADEGAN	Deadly Saber	LIGHTSABER
All Repulse Ranks	DATHOMIR		

COMBOS

Pause the game and select Input Code. Here you can enter the following codes. Activating any of the following cheat codes will disable some unlockables, and you will be unable to save your progress.

COMBO	CODE	COMBO	CODE
All Combos	MOLDYCROW	Saber Slam	PLOKOON
Aerial Ambush	VENTRESS	Saber Sling	KITFISTO
Aerial Assault	EETHKOTH	Sith Saber Flurry	LUMIYA
Aerial Blast	YADDLE	Sith Slash	DARAGON
Impale	BRUTALSTAB	Sith Throw	SAZEN
Lightning Bomb	MASSASSI	New Combo	FREEDON
Lightning Grenade	RAGNOS	New Combo	MARAJADE

ALL DATABANK ENTRIES

Pause the game and select Input Code. Enter OSSUS.

MIRRORED LEVEL

Pause the game and select Input Code. Enter MINDTRICK. Re-enter the code to return level to normal.

SITH MASTER DIFFICULTY

Pause the game and select Input Code. Enter SITHSPAWN.

COSTUMES

Pause the game and select Input Code. Here you can enter the following codes.

COSTUME	CODE	COSTUME	CODE
All Costumes	SOHNDANN	Master Kento	WOOKIEE
Bail Organa	VICEROY	Proxy	PROTOTYPE
Ceremonial Jedi Robes	DANTOOINE	Scout Trooper	FERRAL
Drunken Kota	HARDBOILED	Shadow Trooper	BLACKHOLE
Emperor	MASTERMIND	Sith Stalker Armor	KORRIBAN
Incinerator Trooper	PHOENIX	Snowtrooper	SNOWMAN
Jedi Adventure Robe	HOLOCRON	Stormtrooper	TK421WHITE
Kashyyyk Trooper	TK421GREEN	Stormtrooper Commander	TK421BLUE
Kota	MANDALORE		

STAR WARS THE CLONE WARS: REPUBLIC HEROES

ULTIMATE LIGHTSABER

Pause the game, select Cheats from the Shop, and press Right, Down, Down, Up, Left, Up, Up, Down.

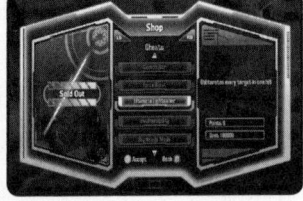 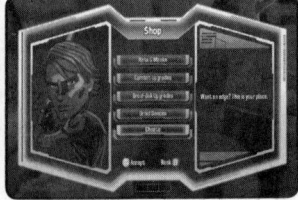

STUNTMAN IGNITION

3 PROPS IN STUNT CREATOR MODE
Select Cheats from Extras and enter COOLPROP.

ALL ITEMS UNLOCKED FOR CONSTRUCTION MODE
Select Cheats from Extras and enter NOBLEMAN.

 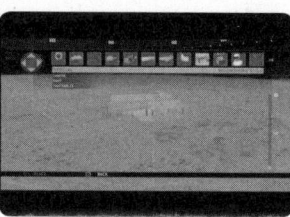

MVX SPARTAN
Select Cheats from Extras and enter fastride.

ALL CHEATS
Select Cheats from Extras and enter Wearefrozen. This unlocks the following cheats: Slo-mo Cool, Thrill Cam, Vision Switcher, Nitro Addiction, Freaky Fast, and Ice Wheels.

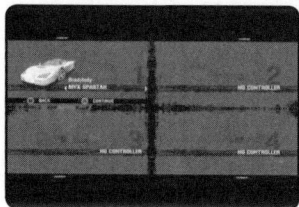 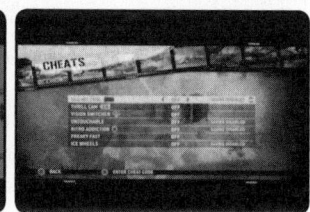

ALL CHEATS
Select Cheats from Extras and enter Kungfoopete.

ICE WHEELS CHEAT
Select Cheats from Extras and enter IceAge.

NITRO ADDICTION CHEAT
Select Cheats from Extras and enter TheDuke.

VISION SWITCHER CHEAT
Select Cheats from Extras and enter GFXMODES.

SUPER CONTRA

UNLIMITED LIVES AND SUPER MACHINEGUN
At the Main menu, select Arcade Game, and then press Up, Up, Down, Down, Left, Right, Left, Right, Ⓑ, Ⓐ. Achievements and the Leaderboard are disabled with this code.

SUPERMAN RETURNS: THE VIDEOGAME

GOD MODE
Pause the game, select Options and press Up, Up, Down, Down, Left, Right, Left, Right, Ⓨ, Ⓧ.

INFINITE CITY HEALTH
Pause the game, select Options and press Ⓨ, Right, Ⓨ, Right, Up, Left, Right, Ⓨ.

ALL POWER-UPS
Pause the game, select Options and press Left, Ⓨ, Right, Ⓧ, Down, Ⓨ, Up, Down, Ⓧ, Ⓨ, Ⓧ.

ALL UNLOCKABLES
Pause the game, select Options and press Left, Up, Right, Down, Ⓨ, Ⓧ, Ⓨ Up, Right, Ⓧ.

FREE ROAM AS BIZARRO
Pause the game, select Options and press Up, Right, Down, Right, Up, Left, Down, Right, Up.

SUPER PUZZLE FIGHTER II TURBO HD REMIX

PLAY AS AKUMA
At the Character Select screen, highlight Hsien-Ko and press Down.

PLAY AS DAN
At the Character Select screen, highlight Donovan and press Down.

PLAY AS DEVILOT
At the Character Select screen, highlight Morrigan and press Down.

PLAY AS ANITA
At the Character Select screen, hold Left Bumper + Right Bumper and choose Donovan.

PLAY AS HSIEN-KO'S TALISMAN
At the Character Select screen, hold Left Bumper + Right Bumper and choose Hsien-Ko.

PLAY AS MORRIGAN AS A BAT
At the Character Select screen, hold Left Bumper + Right Bumper and choose Morrigan.

SURF'S UP

ALL CHAMPIONSHIP LOCATIONS
Select Cheat Codes from the Extras menu and enter FREEVISIT.

ALL LEAF SLIDE STAGES
Select Cheat Codes from the Extras menu and enter GOINGDOWN.

ALL MULTIPLAYER LEVELS
Select Cheat Codes from the Extras menu and enter MULTIPASS.

ALL BOARDS
Select Cheat Codes from the Extras menu and enter MYPRECIOUS.

ASTRAL BOARD
Select Cheat Codes from the Extras menu and enter ASTRAL.

MONSOON BOARD
Select Cheat Codes from the Extras menu and enter MONSOON.

TINE SHOCKWAVE BOARD
Select Cheat Codes from the Extras menu and enter TINYSHOCKWAVE.

ALL CHARACTER CUSTOMIZATIONS

Select Cheat Codes from the Extras menu and enter TOPFASHION.

PLAY AS ARNOLD

Select Cheat Codes from the Extras menu and enter TINYBUTSTRONG.

PLAY AS ELLIOT

Select Cheat Codes from the Extras menu and enter SURPRISEGUEST.

PLAY AS GEEK

Select Cheat Codes from the Extras menu and enter SLOWANDSTEADY.

PLAY AS TANK EVANS

Select Cheat Codes from the Extras menu and enter IMTHEBEST.

PLAY AS TATSUHI KOBAYASHI

Select Cheat Codes from the Extras menu and enter KOBAYASHI.

PLAY AS ZEKE TOPANGA

Select Cheat Codes from the Extras menu and enter THELEGEND.

ALL VIDEOS AND SPEN GALLERY

Select Cheat Codes from the Extras menu and enter WATCHAMOVIE.

ART GALLERY

Select Cheat Codes from the Extras menu and enter NICEPLACE.

THRILLVILLE: OFF THE RAILS

$50,000

While in a park, press Ⓧ, Ⓑ, Ⓨ, Ⓧ, Ⓑ, Ⓨ, Ⓐ.

500 THRILL POINTS

While in a park, press Ⓑ, Ⓧ, Ⓨ, Ⓑ, Ⓧ, Ⓨ, Ⓧ.

ALL PARKS

While in a park, press Ⓧ, Ⓑ, Ⓨ, Ⓧ, Ⓑ, Ⓨ, Ⓧ.

ALL RIDES IN CURRENT PARK

While in a park, press Ⓧ, Ⓑ, Ⓨ, Ⓧ, Ⓑ, Ⓨ, Ⓨ.

MISSION UNLOCK

While in a park, press Ⓧ, Ⓑ, Ⓨ, Ⓧ, Ⓑ, Ⓨ, Ⓑ.

ALL MINI-GAMES IN PARTY PLAY

While in a park, press Ⓧ, Ⓑ, Ⓨ, Ⓧ, Ⓑ, Ⓨ, Right.

TIGER WOODS PGA TOUR 07

BIG HEAD MODE FOR CROWDS

Select Password and enter tengallonhat.

TIGER WOODS PGA TOUR 08

ALL COURSES

Select Password from EA Sports Extras and enter greensfees.

 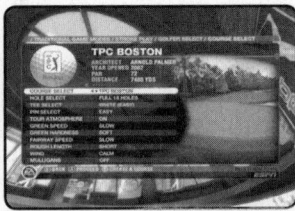

ALL GOLFERS

Select Password from EA Sports Extras and enter allstars.

WAYNE ROONEY

Select Password from EA Sports Extras and enter playfifa08.

INFINITE MONEY

Select Password from EA Sports Extras and enter cream.

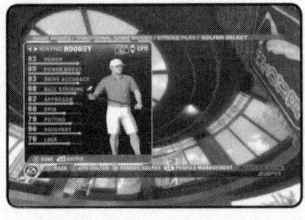 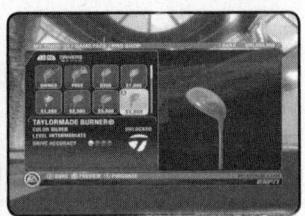

TIGER WOODS PGA TOUR 09

SPECTATORS BIG HEAD MODE

Select EA SPORTS Extras from My Tiger '09, choose Password and enter cephalus.

TMNT

CHALLENGE MAP 2

At the Main menu, hold the Left Bumper and press Ⓐ, Ⓐ, Ⓑ, Ⓐ.

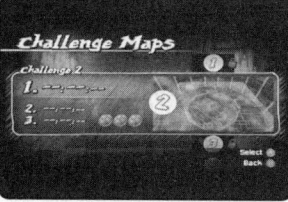

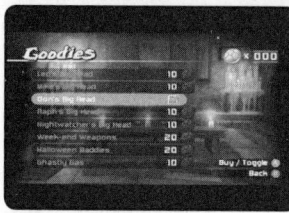

DON'S BIG HEAD GOODIE

At the Main menu, hold the Left Bumper and press Ⓑ, Ⓨ, Ⓐ, Ⓧ.

TOMB RAIDER: LEGEND

The following codes must be unlocked in the game before using them.

BULLETPROOF

During a game, hold Left Trigger and press Ⓐ, Right Trigger, Ⓨ, Right Trigger, Ⓧ, Left Bumper.

DRAIN ENEMY HEALTH

During a game, hold Left Trigger and press Ⓧ, Ⓑ, Ⓐ, Left Bumper, Right Trigger, Ⓨ.

INFINITE ASSAULT RIFLE AMMO

During a game, hold Left Bumper and press Ⓐ, Ⓑ, Ⓐ, Left Trigger, Ⓧ, Ⓨ.

INFINITE GRENADE LAUNCHER AMMO

During a game, hold Left Bumper and press Left Trigger, Ⓨ, Right Trigger, Ⓑ, Left Trigger, Ⓧ

INFINITE SHOTGUN AMMO

During a game, hold Left Bumper and press Right Trigger, Ⓑ, Ⓧ, Left Trigger, Ⓧ, Ⓐ.

INFINITE SMG AMMO

During a game, hold Left Bumper and press Ⓑ, Ⓨ, Left Trigger, Right Trigger, Ⓐ, Ⓑ.

EXCALIBUR

During a game, hold Left Bumper and press Ⓨ, Ⓐ, Ⓑ, Right Trigger, Ⓨ, Left Trigger.

SOUL REAVER

During a game, hold Left Bumper and press Ⓐ, Right Trigger, Ⓑ, Right Trigger, Left Trigger, Ⓧ.

ONE-SHOT KILL

During a game, hold Left Trigger and press Ⓨ, Ⓐ, Ⓨ, Ⓧ, Left Bumper, Ⓑ.

TEXTURELESS MODE

During a game, hold Left Trigger and press Left Bumper, Ⓐ, Ⓑ, Ⓐ, Ⓨ, Right Trigger.

TOM CLANCY'S GHOST RECON ADVANCED WARFIGHTER

ALL MISSIONS

At the Mission Select screen, hold Back + Left Trigger + Right Trigger and press **Y**, Right Bumper, **Y**, Right Bumper, **X**.

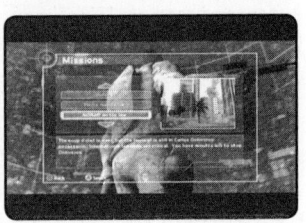

FULL HEALTH

Pause the game, hold Back + Left Trigger + Right Trigger and press Left Bumper, Left Bumper, Right Bumper, **X**, Right Bumper, **Y**.

INVINCIBLE

Pause the game, hold Back + Left Trigger + Right Trigger and press **Y**, **Y**, **X**, Right Bumper, **X**, Left Bumper.

TEAM INVINCIBLE

Pause the game, hold Back + Left Trigger + Right Trigger and press **X**, **X**, **Y**, Right Bumper, **Y**, Left Bumper.

UNLIMITED AMMO

Pause the game, hold Back + Left Trigger + Right Trigger and press Right Bumper, Right Bumper, Left Bumper, **X**, Left Bumper, **Y**.

TOM CLANCY'S HAWX

A-12 AVENGER II

At the hangar, hold Left Trigger and press **X**, **LB**, **X**, **RB**, **Y**, **X**.

F-18 HARV

At the hangar, hold Left Trigger and press **LB**, **Y**, **LB**, **Y**, **LB**, **X**.

FB-22 STRIKE RAPTOR

At the hangar, hold Left Trigger and press **RB**, **X**, **RB**, **X**, **RB**, **Y**.

TONY HAWK'S PROJECT 8

SPONSOR ITEMS

As you progress through Career mode and move up the rankings, you gain sponsors and each comes with its own Create-a-skater item.

RANK REQUIRED	CAS ITEM UNLOCKED
Rank 040	Adio Kenny V2 Shoes
Rank 050	Quiksilver Hoody 3
Rank 060	Birdhouse Tony Hawk Deck
Rank 080	Vans No Skool Gothic Shoes
Rank 100	Volcom Scallero Jacket
Rank 110	eS Square One Shoes
Rank 120	Almost Watch What You Say Deck
Rank 140	DVS Adage Shoe
Rank 150	Element Illuminate Deck
Rank 160	Etnies Sheckler White Lavender Shoes
Complete Skateshop Goal	Stereo Soundwave Deck

SKATERS

All of the skaters, except for Tony Hawk, must be unlocked by completing challenges in the Career Mode. They are useable in Free Skate and 2 Player modes.

SKATER	HOW THEY ARE UNLOCKED
Tony Hawk	Always UnlocOked
Lyn-z Adams Hawkins	Complete Pro Challenge
Bob Burquist	Complete Pro Challenge
Dustin Dollin	Complete Pro Challenge
Nyjah Huston	Complete Pro Challenge
Bam Margera	Complete Pro Challenge
Rodney Mullen	Complete Pro Challenge
Paul Rodriguez	Complete Pro Challenge
Ryan Sheckler	Complete Pro Challenge
Daewon Song	Complete Pro Challenge
Mike Vallely	Complete Pro Challenge
Stevie Willams	Complete Pro Challenge
Travis Barker	Complete Pro Challenge
Kevin Staab	Complete Pro Challenge
Zombie	Complete Pro Challenge
Christaian Hosoi	Rank #1
Jason Lee	Complete Final Tony Hawk Goal
Photographer	Unlock Shops
Security Guard	Unlock School
Bum	Unlock Car Factory
Beaver Mascot	Unlock High School
Real Estate Agent	Unlock Downtown
Filmer	Unlock High School
Skate Jam Kid	Rank #4
Dad	Rank #1
Colonel	All Gaps
Nerd	Complete School Spirit Goal

CHEAT CODES

Select Cheat Codes from the Options and enter the following codes. In game you can access some codes from the Options menu.

CHEAT CODE	RESULTS
plus44	Unlocks Travis Barker
hohohosoi	Unlocks Christian Hosoi
notmono	Unlocks Jason Lee
mixitup	Unlocks Kevin Staab
strangefellows	Unlocks Dad & Skater Jam Kid
themedia	Unlocks Photog Girl & Filmer
militarymen	Unlocks Colonel & Security Guard
jammypack	Unlocks Always Special
balancegalore	Unlocks Perfect Rail
frontandback	Unlocks Perect Manual
shellshock	Unlocks Unlimited Focus
shescaresme	Unlocks Big Realtor
birdhouse	Unlocks Inkblot deck
allthebest	Full Stats
needaride	All Decks unlocked and free, except for inkblot deck and gamestop deck
yougotitall	All specials unlocked and in player's special list and set as owned in skate shop
wearelosers	Unlocks Nerd and a Bum
manineedadate	Unlocks Beaver Mascot
suckstobedead	Unlocks Officer Dick
HATEDANDPROUD	Unlocks the Vans unlockable item

TONY HAWK'S PROVING GROUND

Select Cheat Codes from the Options and enter the following cheats. Some codes need to be enabled by selecting Cheats from the Options during a game.

UNLOCK	CHEAT
Unlocks Boneman	CRAZYBONEMAN
Unlocks Bosco	MOREMILK
Unlocks Cam	NOTACAMERA
Unlocks Cooper	THECOOP
Unlocks Eddie X	SKETCHY
Unlocks El Patinador	PILEDRIVER
Unlocks Eric	FLYAWAY
Unlocks Mad Dog	RABBIES
Unlocks MCA	INTERGALACTIC
Unlocks Mel	NOTADUDE
Unlocks Rube	LOOKSSMELLY
Unlocks Spence	DAPPER
Unlocks Shayne	MOVERS
Unlocks TV Producer	SHAKER
Unlock FDR	THEPREZPARK
Unlock Lansdowne	THELOCALPARK
Unlock Air & Space Museum	THEINDOORPARK
Unlocks all Fun Items	OVERTHETOP
Unlocks all CAS items	GIVEMESTUFF
Unlocks all Decks	LETSGOSKATE
Unlock all Game Movies	WATCHTHIS
Unlock all Lounge Bling Items	SWEETSTUFF
Unlock all Lounge Themes	LAIDBACKLOUNGE
Unlock all Rigger Pieces	IMGONNABUILD
Unlock all Video Editor Effects	TRIPPY
Unlock all Video Editor Overlays	PUTEMONTOP
All specials unlocked and in player's special list	LOTSOFTRICKS
Full Stats	BEEFEDUP
Give player +50 skill points	NEEDSHELP

The following cheats lock you out of the Leaderboards:

UNLOCK	CHEAT
Unlocks Perfect Manual	STILLAINTFALLIN
Unlocks Perfect Rail	AINTFALLIN
Unlock Super Check	BOOYAH
Unlocks Unlimited Focus	MYOPIC
Unlock Unlimited Slash Grind	SUPERSLASHIN
Unlocks 100% branch completion in NTT	FOREVERNAILED
No Bails	ANDAINTFALLIN

You can not use the Video Editor with the following cheats:

UNLOCK	CHEAT
Invisible Man	THEMISSING
Mini Skater	TINYTATER
No Board	MAGICMAN

TRANSFORMERS: THE GAME

The following cheats disable saving and achievements:

INFINITE HEALTH
At the Main menu, press Left, Left, Up, Left, Right, Down, Right.

INFINITE AMMO
At the Main menu, press Up, Down, Left, Right, Up, Up, Down.

NO MILITARY OR POLICE
At the Main menu, press Right, Left, Right, Left, Right, Left, Right.

ALL MISSIONS
At the Main menu, press Down, Up, Left, Right, Right, Right, Up, Down.

BONUS CYBERTRON MISSIONS
At the Main menu, press Right, Up, Up, Down, Right, Left, Left.

GENERATION 1 SKIN: JAZZ
At the Main menu, press Left, Up, Down, Down, Left, Up, Right.

GENERATION 1 SKIN: MEGATRON
At the Main menu, press Down, Left, Left, Down, Right, Right, Up.

GENERATION 1 SKIN: OPTIMUS PRIME
At the Main menu, press Down, Right, Left, Up, Down, Down, Left.

GENERATION 1 SKIN: ROBOVISION OPTIMUS PRIME
At the Main menu, press Down, Down, Up, Up, Right, Right, Right.

GENERATION 1 SKIN: STARSCREAM
At the Main menu, press Right, Down, Left, Left, Down, Up, Up.

TRANSFORMERS REVENGE OF THE FALLEN

LOW GRAVITY MODE
Select Cheat Code and enter Ⓐ, Ⓧ, Ⓨ, ⓔ, Ⓨ, ⓔ.

NO WEAPON OVERHEAT
Select Cheat Code and enter ⓔ, Ⓧ, Ⓐ, ⓔ, Ⓨ, ⓛⓑ.

ALWAYS IN OVERDRIVE MODE
Select Cheat Code and enter ⓛⓑ, Ⓑ, ⓛⓑ, Ⓐ, Ⓧ, ⓡ.

UNLIMITED TURBO
Select Cheat Code and enter Ⓑ, ⓔ, Ⓧ, ⓡ, Ⓐ, Ⓨ.

NO SPECIAL COOLDOWN TIME
Select Cheat Code and enter ⓡ, Ⓧ, ⓡ, ⓡ, Ⓧ, Ⓐ.

INVINCIBILITY
Select Cheat Code and enter ⓡ, Ⓐ, Ⓧ, ⓔ, Ⓧ, Ⓧ.

133

4X ENERGON FROM DEFEATED ENEMIES
Select Cheat Code and enter Y, X, B, ⊛, A, Y.

INCREASED WEAPON DAMAGE IN ROBOT FORM
Select Cheat Code and enter Y, Y, ⊛, A, LB, Y.

INCREASED WEAPON DAMAGE IN VEHICLE FORM
Select Cheat Code and enter Y, B, RB, X, ⊛, ◐.

MELEE INSTANT KILLS
Select Cheat Code and enter ⊛, A, LB, B, ⊛, LB.

LOWER ENEMY ACCURACY
Select Cheat Code and enter X, ◐, ⊛, ◐, ⊛, RB.

INCREASED ENEMY HEALTH
Select Cheat Code and enter B, X, LB, B, ⊛, Y.

INCREASED ENEMY DAMAGE
Select Cheat Code and enter LB, Y, A, Y, ⊛, ⊛.

INCREASED ENEMY ACCURACY
Select Cheat Code and enter Y, Y, B, A, X, LB.

SPECIAL KILLS ONLY MODE
Select Cheat Code and enter B, B, RB, B, A, ◐.

UNLOCK ALL SHANGHAI MISSIONS AND ZONES
Select Cheat Code and enter Y, ◐, ⊛, LB, Y, A.

UNLOCK ALL WEST COAST MISSIONS AND ZONES
Select Cheat Code and enter LB, RB, ⊛, Y, ⊛, B.

UNLOCK ALL DEEP SIX MISSIONS AND ZONES
Select Cheat Code and enter X, RB, Y, B, A, LB.

UNLOCK ALL EAST COAST MISSIONS AND ZONES
Select Cheat Code and enter ⊛, ◐, RB, A, B, X.

UNLOCK ALL CAIRO MISSIONS AND ZONES
Select Cheat Code and enter ⊛, Y, A, Y, ◐, LB.

UNLOCK AND ACTIVATE ALL UPGRADES
Select Cheat Code and enter LB, Y, LB, B, X, X.

UNDERTOW

GAMER PIC 1 – SCUBA DIVER
Total 100 kills.

GAMER PIC 2 – ATLANTIS MAN
Total 10,000 kills.

VIRTUA TENNIS 3

KING & DUKE
At the Main menu, press Up, Up, Down, Down, Left, Right, Left, **LB**, **RB**.

ALL GEAR
At the Main menu, press Left, Right, **B**, Left, Right, **B**, Up, Down.

ALL COURTS
At the Main menu, press Up, Up, Down, Down, Left, Right, Left, Right.

WIN ONE MATCH TO WIN TOURNAMENT
At the Main menu, press **B**, Left, **B**, Right, **B**, Up, **B**, Down.

VIVA PINATA

NEW ITEMS IN PET STORE
Select New Garden and enter chewnicorn as the name.

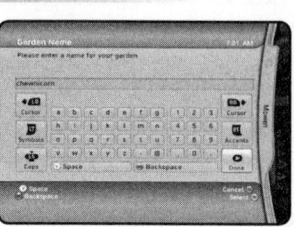

NEW ITEMS IN PET STORE
Select New Garden and enter bullseye as the name.

NEW ITEMS IN PET STORE
Select New Garden and enter goobaa as the name.

NEW ITEMS IN PET STORE
Select New Garden and enter kittyfloss as the name.

VIVA PINATA: PARTY ANIMALS

CLASSIC GAMER AWARD ACHIEVEMENT
At the START screen, press Up, Up, Down, Down, Left, Right, Left, Right, **B**, **A**. This earns you 10 points toward your Gamerscore.

VIVA PINATA: TROUBLE IN PARADISE

CREDITS
Select Play Garden and name your garden Piñata People. This unlocks the ability to view the credits on the main menu.

WALL-E

The following cheats will disable saving. The five possible characters starting with Wall-E and going down are: Wall-E, Auto, EVE, M-O, GEL-A Steward.

ALL BONUS FEATURES UNLOCKED
Select Cheats from the Bonus Features menu and enter Wall-E, Auto, EVE, GEL-A Steward.

ALL GAME CONTENT UNLOCKED
Select Cheats from the Bonus Features menu and enter M-O, Auto, GEL-A Steward, EVE.

ALL SINGLE-PLAYER LEVELS UNLOCKED

Select Cheats from the Bonus Features menu and enter Auto, GEL-A Steward, M-O, Wall-E.

ALL MULTIPLAYER MAPS UNLOCKED

Select Cheats from the Bonus Features menu and enter EVE, M-O, Wall-E, Auto.

ALL HOLIDAY COSTUMES UNLOCKED

Select Cheats from the Bonus Features menu and enter Auto, Auto, GEL-A Steward, GEL-A Steward.

ALL MULTIPLAYER COSTUMES UNLOCKED

Select Cheats from the Bonus Features menu and enter GEL-A Steward, Wall-E, M-O, Auto.

UNLIMITED HEALTH UNLOCKED

Select Cheats from the Bonus Features menu and enter Wall-E, M-O, Auto, M-O.

WALL-E: MAKE ANY CUBE AT ANY TIME

Select Cheats from the Bonus Features menu and enter Auto, M-O, Auto, M-O.

WALL-EVE: MAKE ANY CUBE AT ANY TIME

Select Cheats from the Bonus Features menu and enter M-O, GEL-A Steward, EVE, EVE.

WALL-E WITH A LASER GUN AT ANY TIME

Select Cheats from the Bonus Features menu and enter Wall-E, EVE, EVE, Wall-E.

WALL-EVE WITH A LASER GUN AT ANY TIME

Select Cheats from the Bonus Features menu and enter GEL-A Steward, EVE, M-O, Wall-E.

WALL-E: PERMANENT SUPER LASER UPGRADE

Select Cheats from the Bonus Features menu and enter Wall-E, Auto, EVE, M-O.

EVE: PERMANENT SUPER LASER UPGRADE

Select Cheats from the Bonus Features menu and enter EVE, Wall-E, Wall-E, Auto.

CREDITS

Select Cheats from the Bonus Features menu and enter Auto, Wall-E, GEL-A Steward, M-O.

WWE SMACKDOWN! VS. RAW 2008

HBK AND HHH'S DX OUTFIT

Select Cheat Codes from the Options and enter DXCostume69K2.

KELLY KELLY'S ALTERNATE OUTFIT

Select Cheat Codes from the Options and enter KellyKG12R.

BRET HART

Complete the March 31, 1996 Hall of Fame challenge by defeating Bret Hart with Shawn Michaels in a One-On-One 30-Minute Iron Man Match on Legend difficulty. Purchase from WWE Shop for $210,000.

MICK FOLEY

Complete the June 28, 1998 Hall of Fame challenge by defeating Mick Foley with The Undertaker in a H*** In a Cell Match on Legend difficulty. Purchase from WWE Shop for $210,000.

MR. MCMAHON

Win or successfully defend a championship (WWE or World Heavyweight) at WrestleMania in WWE 24/7 GM Mode. Purchase from WWE Shop for $110,000.

THE ROCK

Complete the April 1, 2001 Hall of Fame challenge by defeating The Rock with Steve Austin in a Single Match on Legend Difficulty. Purchase from WWE Shop for $210,000.

STEVE AUSTIN

Complete the March 23, 1997 Hall of Fame challenge by defeating Steve Austin with Bret Hart in a Submission Match on Legend Difficulty. Purchase from WWE Shop for $210,000.

TERRY FUNK

Complete the April 13, 1997 Hall of Fame challenge by defeating Tommy Dreamer, Sabu and Sandman with any Superstar in an ECW Extreme Rules 4-Way Match on Legend difficulty. Purchase from WWE Shop for $210,000.

MR. MCMAHON BALD

Must unlock Mr. McMahon as a playable character first. Purchase from WWE Shop for $60,000.

WWE SMACKDOWN VS. RAW 2009

BOOGEYMAN

Select Cheat Codes from My WWE and enter BoogeymanEatsWorms!!.

GENE SNITSKY

Select Cheat Codes from My WWE and enter UnlockSnitskySvR2009.

HAWKINS & RYDER

Select Cheat Codes from My WWE and enter Ryder&HawkinsTagTeam.

JILLIAN HALL

Select Cheat Codes from My WWE and enter PlayAsJillianHallSvR.

LAYLA

Select Cheat Codes from My WWE and enter UnlockECWDivaLayla09.

RIC FLAIR

Select Cheat Codes from My WWE and enter FlairWooooooooooooooo.

TAZZ

Select Cheat Codes from My WWE and enter UnlockECWTazzSvR2009.

VINCENT MCMAHON

Select Cheat Codes from My WWE and enter VinceMcMahonNoChance.

HORNSWOGGLE AS MANAGER

Select Cheat Codes from My WWE and enter HornswoggleAsManager.

CHRIS JERICHO COSTUME B

Select Cheat Codes from My WWE and enter AltJerichoModelSvR09.

CM PUNK COSTUME B

Select Cheat Codes from My WWE and enter CMPunkAltCostumeSvR!.

REY MYSTERIO COSTUME B

Select Cheat Codes from My WWE and enter BooyakaBooyaka619SvR.

SATURDAY NIGHT'S MAIN EVENT ARENA

Select Cheat Codes from My WWE and enter SatNightMainEventSvR.

WWE SMACKDOWN VS. RAW 2010

THE ROCK

Select Cheat Codes from the Options menu and enter The Great One.

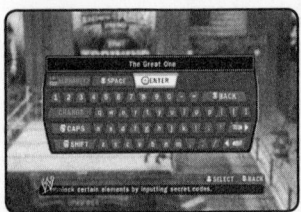
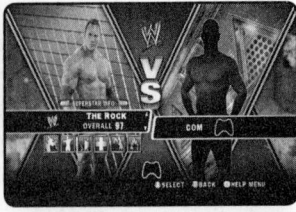

DIRT SHEET BRAWL AND OFFICE STAGE BRAWL

Select Cheat Codes from the Options menu and enter BonusBrawl.

SHAWN MICHAELS' NEW COSTUME

Select Cheat Codes from the Options menu and enter Bow Down.

RANDY ORTON'S NEW COSTUME

Select Cheat Codes from the Options menu and enter ViperRKO.

TRIPLE H'S NEW COSTUME

Select Cheat Codes from the Options menu and enter Suck IT!.

YOU'RE IN THE MOVIES

ALL TRAILERS AND DIRECTOR'S MODE

At the options screen, press Left Bumper, Right Bumper, Left Bumper, Right Bumper, **Y**.

PLAYSTATION® 2

CONTENTS

ASTRO BOY: THE VIDEO GAME

INVULNERABLE
Pause the game and press Up, Down, Down, Up, L1, R1.

MAX STATS
Pause the game and press Left, Left, R1, Down, Down, L1.

INFINITE SUPERS
Pause the game and press Left, L1, Right, L1, Up, Down.

INFINITE DASHES
Pause the game and press R1, R1, L1, R1, Left, Up.

DISABLE SUPERS
Pause the game and press L1, L1, R1, R1, L1, Left.

COSTUME SWAP (ARENA AND CLASSIC COSTUMES)
Pause the game and press R1, Up, L1, Up, Down, R1.

UNLOCK LEVELS
Pause the game and press Up, L1, Right, L1, Down, L1. This allows you to travel to any level from the Story menu.

AVATAR: THE LAST AIRBENDER-THE BURNING EARTH

1 HIT DISHONOR
At the Main menu, press **L1** and select Code Entry. Enter 28260.

ALL BONUS GAME
At the Main menu, press **L1** and select Code Entry. Enter 99801.

ALL GALLERY ITEMS
At the Main menu, press **L1** and select Code Entry. Enter 85061.

DOUBLE DAMAGE
At the Main menu, press **L1** and select Code Entry. Enter 90210.

INFINITE HEALTH
At the Main menu, press **L1** and select Code Entry. Enter 65049.

MAX LEVEL
At the Main menu, press **L1** and select Code Entry. Enter 89121.

UNLIMITED SPECIAL ATTACKS
At the Main menu, press **L1** and select Code Entry. Enter 66206.

AVATAR – THE LAST AIRBENDER: INTO THE INFERNO

ALL CHAPTERS
Select Game Secrets at Ember Islands and enter 52993833.

MAX COINS
Select Game Secrets at Ember Islands and enter 66639224.

ALL ITEMS AVAILABLE AT SHOP
Select Game Secrets at Ember Islands and enter 34737253.

ALL CONCEPT ART
Select Game Secrets at Ember Islands and enter 27858343.

BEN 10: ALIEN FORCE THE GAME

LEVEL LORD
Enter Gwen, Kevin, Big Chill, Gwen as a code.

INVINCIBILITY
Enter Kevin, Big Chill, Swampfire, Kevin as a code.

ALL COMBOS
Enter Swampfire, Gwen, Kevin, Ben as a code.

INFINITE ALIENS
Enter Ben, Swampfire, Gwen, Big Chill as a code.

BEN 10: PROTECTOR OF EARTH

INVINCIBILITY
Select a game from the Continue option. Go to the Map Selection screen, press Start and choose Extras. Select Enter Secret Code and enter XLR8, Heatblast, Wildvine, Fourarms.

ALL COMBOS
Select a game from the Continue option. Go to the Map Selection screen, press Start and choose Extras. Select Enter Secret Code and enter Cannonblot, Heatblast, Fourarms, Heatblast.

ALL LOCATIONS
Select a game from the Continue option. Go to the Map Selection screen, press Start and choose Extras. Select Enter Secret Code and enter Heatblast, XLR8, XLR8, Cannonblot.

DNA FORCE SKINS
Select a game from the Continue option. Go to the Map Selection screen, press Start and choose Extras. Select Enter Secret Code and enter Wildvine, Fourarms, Heatblast, Cannonbolt.

DARK HEROES SKINS
Select a game from the Continue option. Go to the Map Selection screen, press Start and choose Extras. Select Enter Secret Code and enter Cannonbolt, Cannonbolt, Fourarms, Heatblast.

ALL ALIEN FORMS
Select a game from the Continue option. Go to the Map Selection screen, press Start and choose Extras. Select Enter Secret Code and enter Wildvine, Fourarms, Heatblast, Wildvine.

MASTER CONTROL
Select a game from the Continue option. Go to the Map Selection screen, press Start and choose Extras. Select Enter Secret Code and enter Cannonbolt, Heatblast, Wildvine, Fourarms.

BOLT

Some of the following cheats can be toggled on/off by selecting Cheats from the pause menu.

ALL GAME LEVELS
Select Cheats from the Extras menu and enter Right, Up, Left, Right, Up, Right.

ALL MINI GAMES
Select Cheats from the Extras menu and enter Right, Up, Right, Right.

ENCHANCED VISION
Select Cheats from the Extras menu and enter Left, Right, Up, Down.

UNLIMITED GAS MINES
Select Cheats from the Extras menu and enter Right, Left, Left, Up, Down, Right.

UNLIMITED GROUND POUND
Select Cheats from the Extras menu and enter Right, Up, Right, Up, Left, Down.

UNLIMITED INVULNERABILITY

Select Cheats from the Extras menu and enter Down, Down, Up, Left.

UNLIMITED LASER EYES

Select Cheats from the Extras menu and enter Left, Left, Up, Right.

UNLIMITED STEALTH CAMO

Select Cheats from the Extras menu and enter Left, Down, Down, Down.

UNLIMITED SUPERBARK

Select Cheats from the Extras menu and enter Right, Left -Left, Up, Down, Up.

BRATZ: THE MOVIE

FEELIN' PRETTY CLOTHING LINE

In the Bratz office at the laptop computer, enter PRETTY.

HIGH SCHOOL CLOTHING LINE

In the Bratz office at the laptop computer, enter SCHOOL.

PASSION 4 FASHION CLOTHING LINE

In the Bratz office at the laptop computer, enter ANGELZ.

SWEETZ CLOTHING LINE

In the Bratz office at the laptop computer, enter SWEETZ.

CAPCOM CLASSICS COLLECTION VOL. 2

UNLOCK EVERYTHING

At the Title screen, press Left, Right, Up, Down, **L1**, **R1**, **L1**, **R1**. This code unlocks Cheats, Tips, Art, and Sound Tests.

CARS

UNLOCK EVERYTHING

Select Cheat Codes from the Options and enter IF900HP.

ALL CHARACTERS

Select Cheat Codes from the Options and enter YAYCARS.

ALL CHARACTER SKINS

Select Cheat Codes from the Options and enter R4MONE.

ALL MINI-GAMES AND COURSES

Select Cheat Codes from the Options and enter MATTL66.

MATER'S COUNTDOWN CLEAN-UP MINI-GAME AND MATER'S SPEEDY CIRCUIT

Select Cheat Codes from the Options and enter TRGTEXC.

FAST START

Select Cheat Codes from the Options and enter IMSPEED.

INFINITE BOOST

Select Cheat Codes from the Options and enter VROOOOM.

ART

Select Cheat Codes from the Options and enter CONC3PT.

VIDEOS

Select Cheat Codes from the Options and enter WATCHIT.

CARS MATER-NATIONAL

ALL ARCADE RACES, MINI-GAMES, AND WORLDS

Select Codes/Cheats from the options and enter PLAYALL.

ALL CARS

Select Codes/Cheats from the options and enter MATTEL07.

ALTERNATE LIGHTNING MCQUEEN COLORS

Select Codes/Cheats from the options and enter NCEDUDZ.

ALL COLORS FOR OTHERS

Select Codes/Cheats from the options and enter PAINTIT.

UNLIMITED TURBO

Select Codes/Cheats from the options and enter ZZOOOOM.

EXTREME ACCELERATION

Select Codes/Cheats from the options and enter OTO200X.

EXPERT MODE

Select Codes/Cheats from the options and enter VRYFAST.

ALL BONUS ART

Select Codes/Cheats from the options and enter BUYTALL.

CARS RACE-O-RAMA

ALL ARCADE MODE EVENTS

Select Cheats from the Options menu and enter SLVRKEY.

ALL STORY MODE EVENTS

Select Cheats from the Options menu and enter GOLDKEY.

ALL OF LIGHTNING MCQUEEN'S FRIENDS

Select Cheats from the Options menu and enter EVRYBDY.

ALL LIGHTNING MCQUEEN CUSTOM KIT PARTS

Select Cheats from the Options menu and enter GR8MODS.

ALL PAINT JOBS FOR ALL NON-LIGHTNING MCQUEEN CHARACTERS

Select Cheats from the Options menu and enter CARSHOW.

CORALINE

BUTTON EYE CORALINE

Select Cheats from Options and enter Cheese.

CRASH OF THE TITANS

BIG HEAD CRASH

Pause the game, hold **R1**, and press ●, ●, ▲, ✖. Re-enter the code to disable.

SHADOW CRASH

Pause the game, hold **R1**, and press ▲, ●, ▲, ●. Re-enter the code to disable.

THE DA VINCI CODE

GOD MODE

Select Codes from the Options and enter VITRUVIAN MAN.

EXTRA HEALTH

Select Codes from the Options and enter SACRED FEMININE.

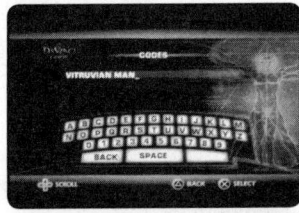

MISSION SELECT

Select Codes from the Options and enter CLOS LUCE 1519.

ONE-HIT FIST KILL

Select Codes from the Options and enter PHILLIPS EXETER.

ONE-HIT WEAPON KILL

Select Codes from the Options and enter ROYAL HOLLOWAY.

ALL VISUAL DATABASE

Select Codes from the Options and enter APOCRYPHA.

ALL VISUAL DATABASE AND CONCEPT ART

Select Codes from the Options and enter ET IN ARCADIA EGO.

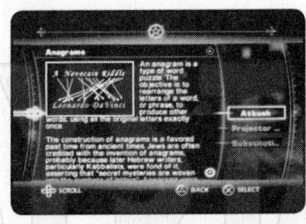

DISNEY PRINCESS: ENCHANTED JOURNEY

BELLE'S KINGDOM
Select Secrets and enter GASTON.

GOLDEN SET
Select Secrets and enter BLUEBIRD.

FLOWER WAND
Select Secrets and enter SLEEPY.

HEART WAND
Select Secrets and enter BASHFUL.

SHELL WAND
Select Secrets and enter RAJAH.

SHIELD WAND
Select Secrets and enter CHIP.

STAR WAND
Select Secrets and enter SNEEZY.

FLATOUT 2

ALL CARS AND 1,000,000 CREDITS
Select Enter Code from the Extras and enter GIEVEPIX.

1,000,000 CREDITS
Select Enter Code from the Extras and enter GIVECASH.

PIMPSTER CAR
Select Enter Code from the Extras and enter RUTTO.

FLATMOBILE CAR
Select Enter Code from the Extras and enter WOTKINS.

MOB CAR
Select Enter Code from the Extras and enter BIGTRUCK.

SCHOOL BUS
Select Enter Code from the Extras and enter GIEVCARPLZ.

ROCKET CAR

Select Enter Code from the Extras and enter KALJAKOPPA.

TRUCK

Select Enter Code from the Extras and enter ELPUEBLO.

G.I. JOE: THE RISE OF COBRA

CLASSIC DUKE

At the main menu, press Left, Up, X, Up, Right, ▲.

CLASSIC SCARLETT

At the main menu, press Right, Up, Down, Down, ▲.

THE GOLDEN COMPASS

The following codes are entered in the order of top/left, bottom/left, top/right. The Featurettes can then be accessed through the Extras menu.

VOICE SESSION 1 FETUREETE

In Extras, select Enter Code from the Game Secrets menu and enter Compass, Sun, Madonna.

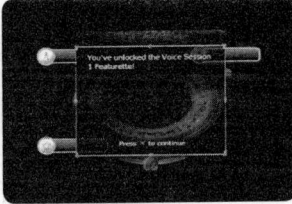

VOICE SESSION 2 FEATURETTE

In Extras, select Enter Code from the Game Secrets menu and enter Compass, Moon, Wild Man.

BEHIND THE SCENES FEATURETTE

In Extras, select Enter Code from the Game Secrets menu and enter Alpha/Omega, Alpha/Omega, Compass.

WILDLIFE WAYSTATION FEATURETTE

In Extras, select Enter Code from the Game Secrets menu and enter Griffin, Elephant, Owl.

POLAR BEARS IN MOTION FEATURETTE

In Extras, select Enter Code from the Game Secrets menu and enter Sun, Moon, Wild Man.

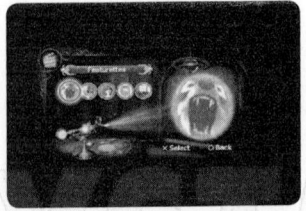

HARRY POTTER AND THE HALF-BLOOD PRINCE

CASTLE GATES ARENA

At the rewards menu, press Right, Right, Down, Down, Left, Right, Left, Right, Left, Right, Start.

ICE AGE 2: THE MELTDOWN

INFINITE PEBBLES

Pause the game and press Down, Down, Left, Up, Up, Right, Up, Down.

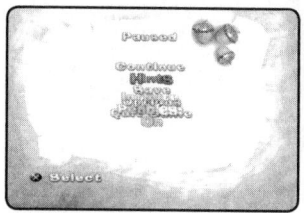 

INFINITE ENERGY

Pause the game and press Down, Left, Right, Down, Down, Right, Left, Down.

INFINITE HEALTH

Pause the game and press Up, Right, Down, Up, Left, Down, Right, Left.

IRON MAN

ARMOR SELECTION

Iron Man's different armor suits are unlocked by completing certain missions. Refer to the following tables for when each is unlocked. After selecting a mission to play, you can pick the armor you wish to use.

COMPLETE MISSION	SUIT UNLOCKED
1: Escape	Mark I
2: First Flight	Mark II
3: Fight Back	Mark III
6: Flying Fortress	Comic Tin Can
9: Home Front	Classic
13: Showdown	Silver Centurion

CONCEPT ART

Concept Art is unlocked after finding certain numbers of Weapon Crates.

CONCEPT ART UNLOCKED	NUMBER OF WEAPON CRATES FOUND
Environments Set 1	6
Environments Set 2	12
Iron Man	18
Environments Set 3	24
Enemies	30
Environments Set 4	36
Villains	42
Vehicles	48
Covers	50

JUICED 2: HOT IMPORT NIGHTS

ASCARI KZ1

Select Cheats and Codes from the DNA Lab menu and enter KNOX. Defeat the challenge to earn the car.

NISSAN SKYLINE R34 GT-R

Select Cheats and Codes from the DNA Lab menu and enter JWRS. Defeat the challenge to earn the car.

KUNG FU PANDA

INVULNERABILITY
Select Cheats from the Extras menu and enter Down, Down, Right, Up, Left.

INFINITE CHI
Select Cheats from the Extras menu and enter Down, Right, Left, Up, Down.

BIG HEAD MODE
Select Cheats from the Extras menu and enter Down, Up, Left, Right, Right.

ALL MULTIPLAYER CHARACTERS
Select Cheats from the Extras menu and enter Left, Down, Left, Right, Down.

DRAGON WARRIOR OUTFIT IN MULTIPLAYER
Select Cheats from the Extras menu and enter Left, Down, Right, Left, Up.

THE LEGEND OF SPYRO: THE ETERNAL NIGHT

INFINITE MAGIC
Pause the game and press Up, Up, Down, Down, Left, Right, Left, Right, L1, R1, L1, R1.

THE LEGEND OF SPYRO: DAWN OF THE DRAGON

INFINITE HEALTH
Pause the game, hold L1 and press Right, Right, Down, Down, Left with the Left Analog Stick.

INFINITE MANA
Pause the game, hold L1 and press Up, Right, Up, Left, Down with the Left Analog Stick.

MAX XP
Pause the game, hold L1 and press Up, Left, Left, Down, Up with the Left Analog Stick.

ALL ELEMENTAL UPGRADES
Pause the game, hold L1 and press Left, Up, Down, Up, Right with the Left Analog Stick.

LEGO BATMAN

BATCAVE CODES
Using the computer in the Batcave, select Enter Code and enter the following codes.

CHARACTERS

CHARACTER	CODE	CHARACTER	CODE
Alfred	ZAQ637	Penguin Henchman	BJH782
Batgirl	JKR331	Penguin Minion	KJP748
Bruce Wayne	BDJ327	Poison Ivy Goon	GTB899
Catwoman (Classic)	M1AAWW	Police Marksman	HKG984
Clown Goon	HJK327	Police Officer	JRY983
Commissioner Gordon	DDP967	Riddler Goon	CRY928
Fishmonger	HGY748	Riddler Henchman	XEU824
Freeze Girl	XVK541	S.W.A.T.	HTF114
Joker Goon	UTF782	Sailor	NAV592
Joker Henchman	YUN924	Scientist	JFL786
Mad Hatter	JCA283	Security Guard	PLB946
Man-Bat	NYU942	The Joker (Tropical)	CCB199
Military Policeman	MKL382	Yeti	NJL412
Nightwing	MVY759	Zoo Sweeper	DWR243
Penguin Goon	NKA238		

VEHICLES

VEHICLE	CODE	VEHICLE	CODE
Bat-Tank	KNTT4B	Mr. Freeze's Kart	BCT229
Bruce Wayne's Private Jet	LEA664	Penguin Goon Submarine	BTN248
Catwoman's Motorcycle	HPL826	Police Bike	LJP234
Garbage Truck	DUS483	Police Boat	PLC999
Goon Helicopter	GCH328	Police Car	KJL832
Harbor Helicopter	CHP735	Police Helicopter	CWR732
Harley Quinn's Hammer Truck	RDT637	Police Van	MAC788
Mad Hatter's Glider	HS000W	Police Watercraft	VJD328
Mad Hatter's Steamboat	M4DM4N	Riddler's Jet	HAHAHA
Mr. Freeze's Iceberg	ICYICE	Robin's Submarine	TTF453
The Joker's Van	JUK657	Two-Face's Armored Truck	EFE933

CHEATS

CHEAT	CODE	CHEAT	CODE
Always Score Multiply	9LRGNB	More Batarang Targets	XWP645
Fast Batarangs	JRBDCB	Piece Detector	KHJ554
Fast Walk	ZOLM6N	Power Brick Detector	MMN786
Flame Batarang	D8NYWH	Regenerate Hearts	HJH7HJ
Freeze Batarang	XPN4NG	Score x2	N4NR3E
Extra Hearts	ML3KHP	Score x4	CX9MAT
Fast Build	EVG26J	Score x6	MLVNF2
Immune to Freeze	JXUDY6	Score x8	WCCDB9
Invincibility	WYD5CP	Score x10	18HW07
Minikit Detector	ZXGH9J		

LEGO STAR WARS II: THE ORIGINAL TRILOGY

BEACH TROOPER

At Mos Eisley Canteena, select Enter Code and enter UCK868. You still need to select Characters and purchase this character for 20,000 studs.

 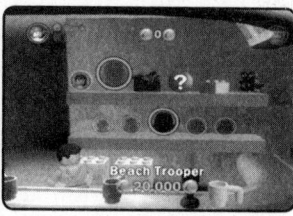

BEN KENOBI (GHOST)

At Mos Eisley Canteena, select Enter Code and enter BEN917. You still need to select Characters and purchase this character for 1,100,000 studs.

BESPIN GUARD

At Mos Eisley Canteena, select Enter Code and enter VHY832. You still need to select Characters and purchase this character for 15,000 studs.

BIB FORTUNA

At Mos Eisley Canteena, select Enter Code and enter WTY721. You still need to select Characters and purchase this character for 16,000 studs.

BOBA FETT

At Mos Eisley Canteena, select Enter Code and enter HLP221. You still need to select
Characters and purchase this character for 175,000 studs.

DEATH STAR TROOPER

At Mos Eisley Canteena, select Enter Code and enter BNC332. You still need to select
Characters and purchase this character for 19,000 studs.

EWOK

At Mos Eisley Canteena, select Enter Code and enter TTT289. You still need to select Characters
and purchase this character for 34,000 studs.

GAMORREAN GUARD

At Mos Eisley Canteena, select Enter Code and enter YZF999. You still need to select
Characters and purchase this character for 40,000 studs.

GONK DROID

At Mos Eisley Canteena, select Enter Code and enter NFX582. You still need to select
Characters and purchase this character for 1,550 studs.

GRAND MOFF TARKIN

At Mos Eisley Canteena, select Enter Code and enter SMG219. You still need to select
Characters and purchase this character for 38,000 studs.

GREEDO

At Mos Eisley Canteena, select Enter Code and enter NAH118. You still need to select
Characters and purchase this character for 60,000 studs.

HAN SOLO (HOOD)

At Mos Eisley Canteena, select Enter Code and enter YWM840. You still need to select
Characters and purchase this character for 20,000 studs.

IG–88

At Mos Eisley Canteena, select Enter Code and enter NXL973. You still need to select
Characters and purchase this character for 30,000 studs.

IMPERIAL GUARD

At Mos Eisley Canteena, select Enter Code and enter MMM111. You still need to select
Characters and purchase this character for 45,000 studs.

IMPERIAL OFFICER

At Mos Eisley Canteena, select Enter Code and enter BBV889. You still need to select
Characters and purchase this character for 28,000 studs.

IMPERIAL SHUTTLE PILOT

At Mos Eisley Canteena, select Enter Code and enter VAP664. You still need to select
Characters and purchase this character for 29,000 studs.

IMPERIAL SPY

At Mos Eisley Canteena, select Enter Code and enter CVT125. You still need to select
Characters and purchase this character for 13,500 studs.

JAWA

At Mos Eisley Canteena, select Enter Code and enter JAW499. You still need to select
Characters and purchase this character for 24,000 studs.

LOBOT

At Mos Eisley Canteena, select Enter Code and enter UUB319. You still need to select Characters and purchase this character for 11,000 studs.

PALACE GUARD

At Mos Eisley Canteena, select Enter Code and enter SGE549. You still need to select Characters and purchase this character for 14,000 studs.

REBEL PILOT

At Mos Eisley Canteena, select Enter Code and enter CYG336. You still need to select Characters and purchase this character for 15,000 studs.

REBEL TROOPER (HOTH)

At Mos Eisley Canteena, select Enter Code and enter EKU849. You still need to select Characters and purchase this character for 16,000 studs.

SANDTROOPER

At Mos Eisley Canteena, select Enter Code and enter YDV451. You still need to select Characters and purchase this character for 14,000 studs.

SKIFF GUARD

At Mos Eisley Canteena, select Enter Code and enter GBU888. You still need to select Characters and purchase this character for 12,000 studs.

SNOWTROOPER

At Mos Eisley Canteena, select Enter Code and enter NYU989. You still need to select Characters and purchase this character for 16,000 studs.

STROMTROOPER

At Mos Eisley Canteena, select Enter Code and enter PTR345. You still need to select Characters and purchase this character for 10,000 studs.

THE EMPEROR

At Mos Eisley Canteena, select Enter Code and enter HHY382. You still need to select Characters and purchase this character for 275,000 studs.

TIE FIGHTER

At Mos Eisley Canteena, select Enter Code and enter HDY739. You still need to select Characters and purchase this character for 60,000 studs.

TIE FIGHTER PILOT

At Mos Eisley Canteena, select Enter Code and enter NNZ316. You still need to select Characters and purchase this character for 21,000 studs.

TIE INTERCEPTOR

At Mos Eisley Canteena, select Enter Code and enter QYA828. You still need to select Characters and purchase this character for 40,000 studs.

TUSKEN RAIDER

At Mos Eisley Canteena, select Enter Code and enter PEJ821. You still need to select Characters and purchase this character for 23,000 studs.

UGNAUGHT

At Mos Eisley Canteena, select Enter Code and enter UGN694. You still need to select Characters and purchase this character for 36,000 studs.

LOONEY TUNES: ACME ARSENAL

UNLIMITED AMMUNITION

At the cheats menu, enter Down, Left, Up, Right, Down, Left, Up, Right, Down.

MAJOR LEAGUE BASEBALL 2K8

BIG HEAD MODE

Select Enter Cheat Code from the My 2K8 menu and enter Black Sox. This unlocks the Smart Choice cheat. Go to My Cheats to toggle the cheat on and off.

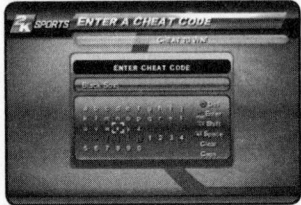 

MAJOR LEAGUE BASEBALL 2K9

BIG HEADS

At the cheats menu, enter Black Sox.

MARVEL SUPER HERO SQUAD

IRON MAN BONUS COSTUMES

Select Enter Code from the Options and enter 111111.

HULK BONUS COSTUMES

Select Enter Code from the Options and enter 222222.

WOLVERINE BONUS COSTUMES

Select Enter Code from the Options and enter 333333.

THOR BONUS COSTUMES

Select Enter Code from the Options and enter 444444.

SILVER SURFER BONUS COSTUMES

Select Enter Code from the Options and enter 555555.

FALCON BONUS COSTUMES

Select Enter Code from the Options and enter 666666.

CHEAT SUPER KNOCKBACK

Select Enter Code from the Options and enter 777777.

CHEAT NO BLOCK MODE

Select Enter Code from the Options and enter 888888.

DR. DOOM BONUS COSTUMES

Select Enter Code from the Options and enter 999999.

MARVEL ULTIMATE ALLIANCE

UNLOCK ALL SKINS
At the Team Menu, press Up, Down, Left, Right, Left, Right, Start.

UNLOCKS ALL HERO POWERS
At the Team Menu, press Left, Right, Up, Down, Up, Down, Start.

UNLOCK ALL HEROES
At the Team Menu, press Up, Up, Down, Down, Left, Left, Left, Start.

UNLOCK DAREDEVIL
At the Team Menu, press Left, Left, Right, Right, Up, Down, Up, Down, Start.

UNLOCK SILVER SURFER
At the Team Menu, press Down, Left, Left, Up, Right, Up, Down, Left, Start.

GOD MODE
During gameplay, press Up, Down, Up, Down, Up, Left, Down, Right, Start.

TOUCH OF DEATH
During gameplay, press Left, Right, Down, Down, Right, Left, Start.

SUPER SPEED
During gameplay, press Up, Left, Up, Right, Down, Right, Start.

FILL MOMENTUM
During gameplay, press Left, Right, Right, Left, Up, Down, Down, Up, Start.

UNLOCK ALL COMICS
At the Review menu, press Left, Right, Right, Left, Up, Up, Right, Start.

UNLOCK ALL CONCEPT ART
At the Review menu, press Down, Down, Down, Right, Right, Left, Down, Start.

UNLOCK ALL MOVIES
At the Review menu, press Up, Left, Left, Up, Right, Right, Up, Start.

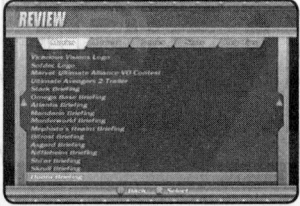

UNLOCK ALL LOAD SCREENS

At the Review menu, press Up, Down, Right, Left, Up, Up Down, Start.

UNLOCK ALL COURSES

At the Comic Missions menu, press Up, Right, Left, Down, Up, Right, Left, Down, Start.

MARVEL: ULTIMATE ALLIANCE 2

GOD MODE

At any point during a game, press Up, Up, Down, Down, Left, Right, Down.

GIVE MONEY

At the Team Select or Hero Details screen press Up, Up, Down, Down, Up, Up, Up, Down.

UNLOCK ALL POWERS

At the Team Select or Hero Details screen press Up, Up, Down, Down, Left, Right, Right, Left.

ADVANCE ALL CHARACTERS TO L99

At the Hero Details screen press Down, Up, Left, Up, Right, Up, Left, Down.

UNLOCK ALL BONUS MISSIONS

While using the Bonus Mission Simulator, press Up, Right, Down, Left, Left, Right, Up, Up.

ADD 1 CHARACTER LEVEL

During a game, press Down, Up, Right, Up, Right, Up, Right, Down.

ADD 10 CHARACTER LEVELS

During a game, press Down, Up, Left, Up, Left, Up, Left, Down.

MLB 07: THE SHOW

CLASSIC STADIUMS

At the Main menu, press Down, Up, Right, Down, Up, Left, Down, Up.

GOLDEN/SLIVER ERA PLAYERS

At the Main menu, press Left, Up, Right, Down, Down, Left, Up, Down.

MLB 08: THE SHOW

ALL CLASSIC STADIUMS

At the main menu, press Down, Right, ●, ●, Left, ▲, Up, L1. The controller will vibrate if entered correctly.

ALL GOLDEN & SILVER ERA PLAYERS IN EXHIBITION

At the main menu, press L1, L2, ●, ●, ▲, ●, Down. The controller will vibrate if entered correctly.

MLB POWER PROS

VIEW MLB PLAYERS AT CREATED PLAYERS MENU

Select View or Delete Custom Players/Password Display from the My Data menu. Press Up, Up, Down, Down, Left, Right, Left Right, L1, R1.

ALVIN LOCKHART'S BATTING STANCE AND PITCHING FORM

At the main menu, press Right, Left, Up, Down, Down, Right, Right, Up, Up, Left, Down, Left. These will be available at the shop.

MVP 07 NCAA BASEBALL

ALL CHALLENGE ITEMS

In Dynasty Mode, create a player with the name David Hamel.

MX VS. ATV UNTAMED

EVERYTHING

Select Cheat Codes from the options menu and enter YOUGOTIT.

1,000,000 STORE POINTS

Select Cheat Codes from the options menu and enter MANYZEROS.

50CC BIKE CLASS

Select Cheat Codes from the options menu and enter LITTLEGUY.

ALL BIKES

Select Cheat Codes from the options menu and enter ONRAILS.

ALL CHALLENGES

Select Cheat Codes from the options menu and enter MORESTUFF.

ALL FREESTYLE TRACKS

Select Cheat Codes from the options menu and enter ALLSTYLE.

ALL GEAR

Select Cheat Codes from the options menu and enter WELLDRESSED.

ALL MACHINES

Select Cheat Codes from the options menu and enter MCREWHEELS.

ALL RIDERS

Select Cheat Codes from the options menu and enter WHOSTHAT.

ALL TRACKS

Select Cheat Codes from the options menu and enter FREETICKET.

MONSTER TRUCK

Select Cheat Codes from the options menu and enter PWNAGE.

NARUTO: ULTIMATE NINJA 2

In Naruto's house, select Input Password. This is where you can enter an element, then three signs. Enter the following here:

1,000 RYO

Water, Hare, Monkey, Monkey
Water, Ram, Horse, Dog
Water, Horse, Horse, Horse
Water, Rat, Rooster, Boar
Water, Rat, Monkey, Rooster
Fire, Rat, Dragon, Dog

5,000 RYO

Water, Tiger, Dragon, Tiger
Water, Snake, Rooster, Horse

10,000 RYO

Fire, Tiger, Tiger, Rooster
Fire, Tiger, Dragon, Hare

NASCAR 08

ALL CHASE MODE CARS

Select Cheat Codes from the Options menu and enter checkered flag.

EA SPORTS CAR

Select Cheat Codes from the Options menu and enter ea sports car.

FANTASY DRIVERS

Select Cheat Codes from the Options menu and enter race the pack.

WALMART CAR AND TRACK

Select Cheat Codes from the Options menu and enter walmart everyday.

NASCAR 09

WALMART TRACK AND THE WALMART CAR

In Chase for the Sprint Cup, enter the driver's name as WalMart EveryDay.

NBA 09 THE INSIDE

ALL-STAR 09 EAST

Select Trophy Room from the Options. Press L1, then ●, and enter SHPNV2K699.

ALL-STAR 09 WEST

Select Trophy Room from the Options. Press L1, then ●, and enter K8AV6YMLNF.

ALL TROPHIES

Select Trophy Room from the Options. Press L1, then ●, and enter K@ZZ@@M!.

LA LAKERS LATIN NIGHTS

Select Trophy Room from the Options. Press L1, then ●, and enter NMTWCTC84S.

MIAMI HEAT LATIN NIGHTS

Select Trophy Room from the Options. Press L1, then ●, and enter WCTGSA8SPD.

PHOENIX SUNS LATIN NIGHTS

Select Trophy Room from the Options. Press L1, then ●, and enter LKUTSENFJH.

SAN ANTONIO LATIN NIGHTS

Select Trophy Room from the Options. Press L1, then ●, and enter JFHSY73MYD.

NBA 2K8

2K SPORTS TEAM

Select Codes from the Features menu and enter 2ksports.

NBA DEVELOPMENT TEAM

Select Codes from the Features menu and enter nba2k.

VISUAL CONCEPTS TEAM

Select Codes from the Features menu and enter vcteam.

ABA BALL

Select Codes from the Features menu and enter payrespect.

NBA 2K10

ABA BALL

Select Codes from Options and enter payrespect.

2K SPORTS TEAM

Select Codes from Options and enter 2ksports.

NBA 2K TEAM

Select Codes from Options and enter nba2k.

VISUAL CONCEPTS TEAM

Select Codes from Options and enter vcteam.

NBA LIVE 08

ADIDAS GIL II ZERO SHOE CODES

Select NBA Codes from My NBA Live and enter the following:

SHOES	CODE
Agent Zero	ADGILLIT6BE
Black President	ADGILLIT7BF
Cuba	ADGILLIT4BC
CustOmize Shoe	ADGILLIT5BD
GilWood	ADGILLIT1B9
TS Lightswitch Away	ADGILLIT0B8
TS Lightswitch Home	ADGILLIT2BA

NCAA FOOTBALL 08

PENNANT CODES

Go to My Shrine and select Pennants. Press Select and enter the following:

PENNANT	CODE	PENNANT	CODE
#200 1st & 15 Cheat	Thanks	#278 All-Clemson Team	Death Valley
#201 Blink Cheat	For	#279 All-Colorado Team	Glory
#202 Boing Cheat	Registering	#281 All-FSU Team	Uprising
#204 Butter Fingers Cheat	With EA	#282 All-Georgia Team	Hunker Down
#205 Crossed The Line Cheat	Tiburon	#283 All-Iowa Team	On Iowa
#206 Cuffed Cheat	EA Sports	#285 All-LSU Team	Geaux Tigers
#207 Extra Credit Cheat	Touchdown	#287 All-Michigan Team	Go Blue
#208 Helium Cheat	In The Zone	#288 All-Mississippi State Team	Hail State
#209 Hurricane Cheat	Turnover	#289 All-Nebraska Team	Go Big Red
#210 Instant FrePlay Cheat	Impact	#291 All-Notre Dame Team	Golden Domer
#211 Jumbalaya Cheat	Heisman	#292 All-Ohio State Team	Killer Nuts
#212 Molasses Cheat	Game Time	#293 All-Oklahoma Team	Boomer
#213 Nike Free Cheat	Break Free	#294 All-Oklahoma State Team	Go Pokes
#214 Nike Magnigrip Cheat	Hand Picked	#296 All-Penn State Team	We Are
#215 Nike Pro Cheat	No Sweat	#298 All-Purdue Team	Boiler Up
#219 QB Dud Cheat	Elite 11	#300 All-Tennessee Team	Big Orange
#221 Steel Toe Cheat	Gridiron	#301 All-Texas Team	Hook Em
#222 Stiffed Cheat	NCAA	#302 All-Texas A&M Team	Gig Em
#223 Super Dive Cheat	Upset	#303 All-UCLA Team	Mighty
#226 Tough As Nail Cheat	Offense	#304 All-USC Team	Fight On
#228 What A Hit Cheat	Blitz	#305 All-Virginia Team	Wahoos
#229 Kicker Hex Cheat	Sideline	#307 All-Washington Team	Bow Down
#273 2004 All-American Team	Fumble	#308 All-Wisconsin Team	U Rah Rah
#274 All-Alabama Team	Roll Tide	#344 MSU Mascot Team	Mizzou Rah
#276 All-Arkansas Team	Woopigsooie	#385 Wyo Mascot	All Hail
#277 All-Auburn Team	War Eagle	#386 Zips Mascot	Hail WV

NEED FOR SPEED PROSTREET

$2,000
Select Career and then choose Code Entry. Enter 1MA9X99.

$4,000
Select Career and then choose Code Entry. Enter W2IOLL01.

$8,000
Select Career and then choose Code Entry. Enter L1IS97A1.

$10,000
Select Career and then choose Code Entry. Enter 1MI9K7E1.

$10,000
Select Career and then choose Code Entry. Enter CASHMONEY.

$10,000
Select Career and then choose Code Entry. Enter REGGAME.

AUDI TT
Select Career and then choose Code Entry. Enter ITSABOUTYOU.

CHEVELLE SS
Select Career and then choose Code Entry. Enter HORSEPOWER.

COKE ZERO GOLF GTI
Select Career and then choose Code Entry. Enter COKEZERO.

DODGE VIPER
Select Career and then choose Code Entry. Enter WORLDSLONGESTLASTING.

MITSUBISHI LANCER EVOLUTION
Select Career and then choose Code Entry. Enter MITSUBISHIGOFAR.

UNLOCK ALL BONUSES
Select Career and then choose Code Entry. Enter UNLOCKALLTHINGS.

5 REPAIR MARKERS
Select Career and then choose Code Entry. Enter SAFETYNET.

ENERGIZER VINYL
Select Career and then choose Code Entry. Enter ENERGIZERLITHIUM.

CASTROL SYNTEC VINYL
Select Career and then choose Code Entry. Enter CASTROLSYNTEC. This also gives you
$10,000.

NHL 08

ALL RBK EDGE JERSEYS
At the RBK Edge Code option, enter h3oyxpwksf8ibcgt.

NHL 09

UNLOCK 3RD JERSEYS
At the cheat menu, enter xe6377uyrwm48frf.

NICKTOONS: ATTACK OF THE TOYBOTS

DAMAGE BOOST
Select Cheats from the Extras menu. Choose Enter Cheat Code and enter 456645.

INVULNERABILITY
Select Cheats from the Extras menu. Choose Enter Cheat Code and enter 313456.

UNLOCK EXO-HUGGLES 9000
Select Cheats from the Extras menu. Choose Enter Cheat Code and enter 691427.

UNLOCK MR. HUGGLES
Select Cheats from the Extras menu. Choose Enter Cheat Code and enter 654168.

UNLIMITED LOBBER GOO
Select Cheats from the Extras menu. Choose Enter Cheat Code and enter 118147.

UNLIMITED SCATTER GOO
Select Cheats from the Extras menu. Choose Enter Cheat Code and enter 971238.

UNLIMITED SPLITTER GOO
Select Cheats from the Extras menu. Choose Enter Cheat Code and enter 854511.

RATATOUILLE

Select Gusteau's Shop from the Extras menu. Choose Secrets, select the appropriate code number, and then enter the code. Once the code is entered, select the cheat you want to activate it.

 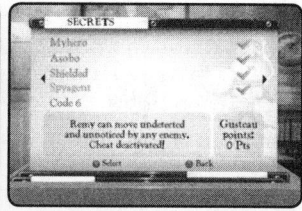

CODE NUMBER	CODE	EFFECT
1	Pieceocake	Very Easy difficulty mode
2	Myhero	No impact and no damage from enemies
3	Asobo	Plays the Asobo logo
4	Shielded	No damage from enemies
5	Spyagent	Move undetected by any enemy
6	Ilikeonions	Release air every time Remy jumps
7	Hardfeelings	Head butt when attacking instead of tailswipe
8	Slumberparty	Multiplayer mode
9	Gusteauart	All Concept Art
10	Gusteauship	All four championship modes
11	Mattelme	All single player and multiplayer mini-games
12	Gusteauvid	All Videos
13	Gusteaures	All Bonus Artworks
14	Gusteaudream	All Dream Worlds in Gusteau's Shop
15	Gusteauslide	All Slides in Gusteau's Shop
16	Gusteaulevel	All single player mini-games
17	Gusteaucombo	All items in Gusteau's Shop
18	Gusteaupot	5,000 Gusteau points
19	Gusteaujack	10,000 Gusteau points
20	Gusteauomni	50,000 Gusteau points

SCOOBY-DOO! FIRST FRIGHTS

DAPHNE'S SECRET COSTUME
Select Codes from the Extras menu and enter 2839.

FRED'S SECRET COSTUME
Select Codes from the Extras menu and enter 4826.

SCOOBY DOO'S SECRET COSTUME
Select Codes from the Extras menu and enter 1585.

SHAGGY'S SECRET COSTUME
Select Codes from the Extras menu and enter 3726.

VELMA'S SECRET COSTUME
Select Codes from the Extras menu and enter 6588.

SEGA SUPERSTARS TENNIS

UNLOCK CHARACTERS
Complete the following missions to unlock the corresponding character.

CHARACTER	MISSION TO COMPLETE
Alex Kidd	Mission 1 of Alex Kidd's World
Amy Rose	Mission 2 of Sonic the Hedgehog's World
Gilius	Mission 1 of Golden Axe's World
Gum	Mission 12 of Jet Grind Radio's World
Meemee	Mission 8 of Super Monkey Ball's World
Pudding	Mission 1 of Space Channel 5's World
Reala	Mission 2 of NiGHTs' World
Shadow The Hedgehog	Mission 14 of Sonic the Hedgehog's World

SHREK THE THIRD

10,000 GOLD COINS
At the gift shop, press Up, Up, Down, Up, Right, Left.

THE SIMPSONS GAME

UNLIMITED POWER FOR ALL CHARACTERS
At the Extras menu, press ◉, Left, Right, ◉, ◉, L1.

ALL CLICHÉS.
At the Extras menu, press Left, ◉, Right, ◉, Right, L1.

ALL MOVIES
At the Extras menu, press ◉, Left, ◉, Right, ◉, R1.

THE SIMS 2: CASTAWAY

CHEAT GNOME
During a game, press **R1**, **L1**, Down, ◉, **R2**. You can now use this Gnome to get the following:

MAX ALL MOTIVES
During a game, press **R2**, Up, X, ◉, **L1**.

MAX CURRENT INVENTORY
During a game, press Left, Right, ◉, **R2**, ◉.

MAX RELATIONSHIPS
During a game, press **L1**, Up, **R2**, Left, ▲.

ALL RESOURCES
During a game, press ◉, ▲, Down, X, Left.

ALL CRAFTING PLANS

During a game, press X, ▲, L2, ●, R1.

ADD 1 TO SKILL

During a game, press ▲, L1, L1, Left, ▲.

EXCLUSIVE VEST AND TANKTOP

Pause the game and go to Fashion and Grooming. Press ●, R2, R2, ▲, Down.

THE SIMS 2: PETS

CHEAT GNOME

During a game, press L1, L1, R1, ✖, ✖, Up.

GIVE SIM PET POINTS

After activating the Cheat Gnome, press ▲, ●, ✖, ●, L1, R1 during a game. Select the Gnome to access the cheat.

ADVANCE 6 HOURS

After activating the Cheat Gnome, press Up, Left, Down, Right, R1 during a game. Select the Gnome to access the cheat.

GIVE SIM SIMOLEONS

After activating the Cheat Gnome, enter the Advance 6 Hours cheat. Access the Gnome and exit. Enter the cheat again. Now, Give Sim Simoleons should be available from the Gnome.

CAT AND DOG CODES

When creating a family, press ● to Enter Unlock Code. Enter the following for new fur patterns.

FUR PATTERN/CAT OR DOG	UNLOCK CODE
Bandit Mask Cats	EEGJ2YRQZZAIZ9QHA64
Bandit Mask Dogs	EEGJ2YRQZQARQ9QHA64
Black Dot Cats	EEGJ2YRZQQ1IQ9QHA64
Black Dot Dogs	EEGJ2YRZQZZ1IQ9QHA64
Black Smiley Cats	EEGJ2YRQQZ1RQ9QHA64
Black Smiley Dogs	EEGJ2YRZQQARQ9QHA64

FUR PATTERN/CAT OR DOG	UNLOCK CODE
Blue Bones Cats	EEGJ2YRQZZARQ9QHA64
Blue Bones Dogs	EEGJ2YRZZZ1IZ9QHA64
Blue Camouflage Cats	EEGJ2YRZZQ1IQ9QHA64
Blue Camouflage Dogs	EEGJ2YRZZZ1RQ9QHA64
Blue Cats	EEGJ2YRQZZAIQ9QHA64
Blue Dogs	EEGJ2YRQQQ1IZ9QHA64
Blue Star Cats	EEGJ2YRQQZ1IZ9QHA64
Blue Star Dogs	EEGJ2YRZZQ1IQ9QHA64
Deep Red Cats	EEGJ2YRQQQAIQ9QHA64
Deep Red Dogs	EEGJ2YRQZQ1RQ9QHA64
Goofy Cats	EEGJ2YRQZQ1IZ9QHA64
Goofy Dogs	EEGJ2YRZZZARQ9QHA64
Green Cats	EEGJ2YRZQQAIZ9QHA64
Green Dogs	EEGJ2YRQZQAIQ9QHA64
Green Flower Cats	EEGJ2YRZQZAIQ9QHA64
Green Flower Dogs	EEGJ2YRQZZ1RQ9QHA64
Light Green Cats	EEGJ2YRZZQ1RQ9QHA64
Light Green Dogs	EEGJ2YRZQQQ1RQ9QHA64
Navy Hearts Cats	EEGJ2YRZQZ1IQ9QHA64
Navy Hearts Dogs	EEGJ2YRQQZ1IQ9QHA64
Neon Green Cats	EEGJ2YRZZQAIQ9QHA64
Neon Green Dogs	EEGJ2YRZQQAIQ9QHA64
Neon Yellow Cats	EEGJ2YRZZQARQ9QHA64
Neon Yellow Dogs	EEGJ2YRQQQAIZ9QHA64
Orange Diagonal Cats	EEGJ2YRQQZAIQ9QHA64
Orange Diagonal Dogs	EEGJ2YRZQZ1IZ9QHA64
Panda Cats	EEGJ2YRQZQAIZ9QHA64
Pink Cats	EEGJ2YRQZZ1IZ9QHA64
Pink Dogs	EEGJ2YRZQZ1RQ9QHA64
Pink Vertical Strip Cats	EEGJ2YRQQQARQ9QHA64
Pink Vertical Strip Dogs	EEGJ2YRZZZAIQ9QHA64
Purple Cats	EEGJ2YRQQZARQ9QHA64
Purple Dogs	EEGJ2YRQQZAIZ9QHA64
Star Cats	EEGJ2YRZQZARQ9QHA64
Star Dogs	EEGJ2YRZQZAIZ9QHA64
White Paws Cats	EEGJ2YRQQQ1RQ9QHA64
White Paws Dogs	EEGJ2YRZQQ1IZ9QHA64
White Zebra Stripe Cats	EEGJ2YRZZQ1IZ9QHA64
White Zebra Stripe Dogs	EEGJ2YRZZZ1IQ9QHA64
Zebra Stripes Dogs	EEGJ2YRZZQAIZ9QHA64

SLY 3: HONOR AMONG THIEVES

TOONAMI PLANE

While flying the regular plane, pause the game and press **R1**, **R1**, Right, Down, Down, Right.

RESTART EPISODES

Pause the game during the Episode and enter the following codes to restart that Episode. You must first complete that part of the Episode to use the code.

EPISODE	CODE
Episode 1, Day 1	Left, R2, Right, L1, R2, L1
Episode 1, Day 2	Down, L2, Up, Left, R2, L2
Episode 2, Day 1	Right, L2, Left, Up, Right, Down
Episode 2, Day 2	Down, Up, R1, Up, R2, L2
Episode 3, Day 1	R2, R1, L1, Left, L1, Down
Episode 3, Day 2	L2, R1, R2, L2, L1, Up

EPISODE	CODE
Episode 4, Day 1	Left, Right, L1, R2, Right, R2
Episode 4, Day 2	L1, Left, L2, Left, Up, L1
Episode 5, Day 1	Left, R2, Right, Up, L1, R2
Episode 5, Day 2	R2, R1, L1, R1, R2, R1
Operation Laptop Retrieval	L2, Left, R1, L2, L1, Down
Operation Moon Crash	L2, Up, Left, L1, L2, L1
Operation Reverse Double Cross	Right, Left, Up, Left, R2, Left
Operation Tar Be-Gone	Down, L2, R1, L2, R1, Right
Operation Turbo Dominant Eagle	Down, Right, Left, L2, R1, Right
Operation Wedding Crasher	L2, R2, Right, Down, L1, R2

SPIDER-MAN: FRIEND OR FOE

NEW GREEN GOBLIN AS A SIDEKICK

While standing in the Helicarrier between levels, press Left, Down, Right, Right, Down, Left.

SANDMAN AS A SIDEKICK

While standing in the Helicarrier between levels, press Right, Right, Right, Up, Down, Left.

VENOM AS A SIDEKICK

While standing in the Helicarrier between levels, press Left, Left, Right, Up, Down, Down.

5000 TECH TOKENS

While standing in the Helicarrier between levels, press Up, Up, Down, Down, Left, Right.

THE SPIDERWICK CHRONICLES

INVULNERABILITY

During the game, hold L1 + R1 and press ▲, ▲, ▲, ▲, ✕, ✕, ▲, ▲.

HEAL

During the game, hold L1 + R1 and press ▲, ●, ✕, ●, ▲, ●, ✕, ●.

COMBAT LOADOUT

During the game, hold L1 + R1 and press ▲, ▲, ✕, ✕, ●, ●, ●, ●.

INFINITE AMMO

During the game, hold L1 + R1 and press ●, ●, ●, ●, ✕, ✕, ✕, ▲.

FIELD GUIDE UNLOCKED

During the game, hold L1 + R1 and press ●, ●, ●, ●, ▲, ▲, ▲, ✕.

SPRITE A

During the game, hold L2 + R2 and press ▲, ✕, ●, ●, ▲, ✕, ●, ●.

SPRITE B

During the game, hold L2 + R2 and press ✕, ✕, ▲, ●, ●, ●, ▲, ✕.

SPRITE C

During the game, hold L2 + R2 and press ●, ▲, ●, ✕, ●, ▲, ●, ✕.

SPONGEBOB SQUAREPANTS FEATURING NICKTOONS: GLOBS OF DOOM

When entering the following codes, the order of the characters going down is: SpongeBob SquarePants, Nicolai Technus, Danny Phantom, Dib, Zim, Tlaloc, Tak, Beautiful Gorgeous, Jimmy Neutron, Plankton. These names are shortened to the first name in the following.

ATTRACT COINS

Using the Upgrade Machine on the bottom level of the lair, select "Input cheat codes here". Enter Tlaloc, Plankton, Danny, Plankton, Tak. Coins are attracted to you making them much easier to collect.

DON'T LOSE COINS

Using the Upgrade Machine on the bottom level of the lair, select "Input cheat codes here". Enter Plankton, Jimmy, Beautiful, Jimmy, Plankton. You don't lose coins when you get knocked out.

GOO HAS NO EFFECT

Using the Upgrade Machine on the bottom level of the lair, select "Input cheat codes here". Enter Danny, Danny, Danny, Nicolai, Nicolai. Goo does not slow you down.

MORE GADGET COMBO TIME

Using the Upgrade Machine on the bottom level of the lair, select "Input cheat codes here". Enter SpongeBob, Beautiful, Danny, Plankton, Nicolai. You have more time to perform gadget combos.

STAR WARS: THE FORCE UNLEASHED

CHEATS

Once you have accessed the Rogue Shadow, select Enter Code from the Extras menu. Now you can enter the following codes:

CHEAT	CODE	CHEAT	CODE
Invincibility	CORTOSIS	Max Force Power Level	KATARN
Unlimited Force	VERGENCE	Max Combo Level	COUNTDOOKU
1,000,000 Force Points	SPEEDER	Stronger Lightsaber	LIGHTSABER
All Force Powers	TYRANUS		

COSTUMES

Once you have accessed the Rogue Shadow, select Enter Code from the Extras menu. Now you can enter the following codes:

COSTUME	CODE	COSTUME	CODE
All Costumes	GRANDMOFF	Juno Eclipse	ECLIPSE
501st Legion	LEGION	Kento's Robe	WOOKIEE
Aayla Secura	AAYLA	Kleef	KLEEF
Admiral Ackbar	ITSATWAP	Lando Calrissian	SCOUNDREL
Anakin Skywalker	CHOSENONE	Luke Skywalker	T16WOMPRAT
Asajj Ventress	ACOLYTE	Luke Skywalker (Yavin)	YELLOWJCKT
Ceremonial Jedi Robes	DANTOOINE	Mace Windu	JEDIMASTER
Chop'aa Notimo	NOTIMO	Mara Jade	MARAJADE
Classic stormtrooper	TK421	Maris Brook	MARISBROOD
Count Dooku	SERENNO	Navy commando	STORMTROOP
Darth Desolous	PAUAN	Obi Wan Kenobi	BENKENOBI
Darth Maul	ZABRAK	Proxy	HOLOGRAM
Darth Phobos	HIDDENFEAR	Qui Gon Jinn	MAVERICK
Darth Vader	SITHLORD	Shaak Ti	TOGRUTA
Drexl Roosh	DREXLROOSH	Shadow trooper	INTHEDARK
Emperor Palpatine	PALPATINE	Sith Robes	HOLOCRON
General Rahm Kota	MANDALORE	Sith Stalker Armor	KORRIBAN
Han Solo	NERFHERDER	Twi'lek	SECURA
Heavy trooper	SHOCKTROOP		

STREET FIGHTER ALPHA

PLAY AS DAN

At the Character Select screen in Arcade Mode, hold the Start button and place the cursor on the Random Select space then input one of the following commands within 1 second:

LP LK MK HK HP MP

HP HK MK LK LP MP

LK LP MP HP HK MK

HK HP MP LP LK HK

PLAY AS M.BISON

At the Character Select screen, hold the Start button, place the cursor on the random select box, and input:

1P side: Down, Down, Back, Back, Down, Back, Back + LP + HP

2P side: Down, Down, Forward, Forward, Down, Forward, Forward + LP + HP

PLAY AS AKUMA

At the Character Select screen, hold the Start button, place the cursor on the random select box, and input:

1P side: Down, Down, Down, Back, Back, Back + LP + HP

2P side: Down, Down, Down, Forward, Forward, Forward + LP + HP

AKUMA MODE

Select your character in Arcade mode, then press and hold Start + MP + MK as the Character Selection screen ends.

RYU AND KEN VS. M.BISON

On both the 1p and 2p side in Arcade mode, press and hold Start, then:

1P side: place the cursor on Ryu and input Up, Up, release Start, Up, Up + LP

2P side: place the cursor on Ken and input Up, Up, release Start, Up, Up + HP

LAST BOSS MODE

Select Arcade mode while holding ⬤, ✖, and **R1**.

DRAMATIC BATTLE MODE

Select Dramatic Battle mode while holding ⬤, ✖, and **R2**.

RANDOM BATTLE MODE

Select Versus mode while holding ⬤, ✖, and **R2**.

STREET FIGHTER ALPHA 2

PLAY AS ORIGINAL CHUN-LI

Highlight Chun-Li on the Character Select screen, hold the Start button for 3 seconds, then select Chun-Li normally.

PLAY AS SHIN AKUMA

Highlight Akuma on the Character Select screen, hold the Start button for 3 seconds, then select Akuma normally.

PLAY AS EVIL RYU

Highlight Ryu on the Character Select screen, hold the Start button, input Forward, Up, Down, Back, then select Ryu normally.

PLAY AS EX DHALSIM

Highlight Dhalsim on the Character Select screen, hold the Start button, input Back, Down, Forward, Up, then select Dhalsim normally.

PLAY AS EX ZANGIEF

Highlight Zangief on the Character Select screen, hold the Start button, input Down, Back, Back, Back, Back, Up, Up, Forward, Forward, Forward, Forward, Down, then select Zangief normally.

LAST BOSS MODE

Select Arcade mode while holding the ●, ●, and R1 buttons.

DRAMATIC BATTLE MODE

Select Dramatic Battle mode while holding the ● + ✕ + R2.

SELECT SPECIAL ROUTE IN SURVIVAL MODE

Select Survival Battle while holding the R1 or R2.

RANDOM BATTLE MODE

Select Versus mode while holding the ● + ✕ + R2.

STREET FIGHTER ALPHA 2 GOLD

PLAY AS EX RYU

Highlight Ryu and press the Start button once before selecting normally.

PLAY AS EVIL RYU

Highlight Ryu and press the Start button twice before selecting normally.

PLAY AS ORIGINAL CHUN-LI

Highlight Chun-Li and press the Start button once before selecting normally.

PLAY AS EX CHUN-LI

Highlight Chun-Li and press the Start button twice before selecting normally.

PLAY AS EX KEN

Highlight Ken and press the Start button once before selecting normally.

PLAY AS EX DHALSIM

Highlight Dhalsim and press the Start button once before selecting normally.

PLAY AS EX ZANGIEF

Highlight Zangief and press the Start button once before selecting normally.

PLAY AS EX SAGAT

Highlight Sagat and press the Start button once before selecting normally.

PLAY AS EX M.BISON

Highlight M.Bison and press the Start button once before selecting normally.

PLAY USING SAKURA'S ALTERNATE COLORS

Highlight Sakura and press the Start button five times before selecting normally.

PLAY AS SHIN AKUMA

Highlight Akuma and press the Start button five times before selecting normally.

PLAY AS CAMMY

Highlight M.Bison and press the Start button twice before selecting normally.

LAST BOSS MODE

Select Arcade mode while holding ● + ● + R1.

SELECT SPECIAL ROUTE IN SURVIVAL MODE
Select Survival Battle while holding the **R1** or **R2**.

DRAMATIC BATTLE MODE
Select Dramatic Battle mode while holding ⬤ + ⊗ + **R2**.

RANDOM BATTLE MODE
Select Versus mode while holding ⬤ + ⊗ + **R2**.

STREET FIGHTER ALPHA 3

PLAY AS BALROG
Highlight Karin for one second, then move the cursor to the random select box and hold Start before selecting normally.

PLAY AS JULI
Highlight Karin for one second, then move the cursor to the random select box and press Up, or Down, while selecting normally.

PLAY AS JUNI
Highlight Karin for one second, then move the cursor to the random select box and press Back, or Forward, while selecting normally.

CLASSICAL MODE
Press and hold HP + HK while starting game.

SPIRITED MODE
Press and hold MP + MK while starting game.

SAIKYO MODE
Press and hold LP + LK while starting game.

SHADALOO MODE
Press and hold LK + MK + HK while starting game.

SELECT SPECIAL ROUTE IN SURVIVAL MODE
Select Survival mode while holding **R1** or **R2**.

DRAMATIC BATTLE MODE
Select Dramatic Battle mode while holding ⬤ + ⊗ + **R2**.

RANDOM BATTLE MODE
Select Versus mode while holding ⬤ + ⊗ + **R2**.

STUNTMAN IGNITION

3 PROPS IN STUNT CREATOR MODE
Select Cheats from Extras and enter COOLPROP.

ALL ITEMS UNLOCKED FOR CONSTRUCTION MODE
Select Cheats from Extras and enter NOBLEMAN.

MVX SPARTAN
Select Cheats from Extras and enter fastride.

ALL CHEATS
Select Cheats from Extras and enter Wearefrozen. This unlocks the following cheats: Slo-mo Cool, Thrill Cam, Vision Switcher, Nitro Addiction, Freaky Fast, and Ice Wheels.

ALL CHEATS
Select Cheats from Extras and enter Kungfoopete.

ICE WHEELS CHEAT

Select Cheats from Extras and enter IceAge.

NITRO ADDICTION CHEAT

Select Cheats from Extras and enter TheDuke.

VISION SWITCHER CHEAT

Select Cheats from Extras and enter GFXMODES.

TAK AND THE GUARDIANS OF GROSS

INVULNERABILITY

Select Cheat Codes from the Extras menu and enter KRUNKIN.

INFINITE NOVA

Select Cheat Codes from the Extras menu and enter CAKEDAY.

WEAK ENEMIES

Select Cheat Codes from the Extras menu and enter CODMODE.

ALL LEVELS

Select Cheat Codes from the Extras menu and enter GUDGEON.

ALL MINI GAMES

Select Cheat Codes from the Extras menu and enter CURLING.

ALL AWARDS

Select Cheat Codes from the Extras menu and enter SNEAKER.

ALL CONCEPT ART

Select Cheat Codes from the Extras menu and enter FRIVERS.

RAINBOW TRAIL

Select Cheat Codes from the Extras menu and enter UNICORN.

TEENAGE MUTANT NINJA TURTLES: SMASH-UP

CYBER SHREDDER

At the Bonus Content menu, press Up, Down, Right, Up, Down, Right, Left, Up, Right, Down.

4 NINJA TURTLES' ALTERNATE COSTUMES

At the Bonus Content menu, press Up, Left, Down, Right, Up, Down, Left, Up, Left, Left.

TIGER WOODS PGA TOUR 08

ALL GOLFERS

Select Passwords from the Options and enter GAMEFACE.

BRIDGESTONE ITEMS

Select Passwords from the Options and enter SHOJIRO.

COBRA ITEMS

Select Passwords from the Options and enter SNAKEKING.

GRAFALLOY ITEMS

Select Passwords from the Options and enter JUSTSHAFTS.

MACGREGOR ITEMS

Select Passwords from the Options and enter MACTEC.

MIZUNO ITEMS

Select Passwords from the Options and enter RIHACHINRIZO.

NIKE ITEMS
Select Passwords from the Options and enter JUSTDOIT.

OAKLEY ITEMS
Select Passwords from the Options and enter JANNARD.

PING ITEMS
Select Passwords from the Options and enter SOLHEIM.

PRECEPT ITEMS
Select Passwords from the Options and enter GUYSAREGOOD.

TAYLORMADE ITEMS
Select Passwords from the Options and enter MRADAMS.

TIGER WOODS PGA TOUR 09

$1,000,000
Select Passwords from the Extras menu and enter JACKPOT.

MAX SKILL POINTS
Select Passwords from the Extras menu and enter IAMRUBBISH.

ALL CLOTHING & EQUIPMENT
Select Passwords from the Extras menu and enter SHOP2DROP.

ALL PGA TOUR EVENTS
Select Passwords from the Extras menu and enter BEATIT.

ALL COVER STORIES
Select Passwords from the Extras menu and enter HEADLINER.

TONY HAWK'S PROVING GROUND

CHEAT CODES
Select Cheat Codes from the Options and enter the following cheats. Some codes need to be enabled by selecting Cheats from the Options during a game.

UNLOCK	CHEAT
Unlocks Bosco	MOREMILK
Unlocks Cam	NOTACAMERA
Unlocks Cooper	THECOOP
Unlocks Eddie X	SKETCHY
Unlocks El Patinador	PILEDRIVER
Unlocks Eric	FLYAWAY
Unlocks Judy Nails	LOVEROCKNROLL
Unlocks Mad Dog	RABBIES
Unlocks MCA	INTERGALACTIC
Unlocks Mel	NOTADUDE
Unlocks Rube	LOOKSSMELLY
Unlocks Spence	DAPPER
Unlocks Shayne	MOVERS
Unlocks TV Producer	SHAKER
Unlock FDR	THEPREZPARK
Unlock Lansdowne	THELOCALPARK
Unlock Air & Space Museum	THEINDOORPARK
Unlocks all Fun Items	OVERTHETOP
Unlock all Game Movies	WATCHTHIS
Unlock all Rigger Pieces	IMGONNABUILD

UNLOCK	CHEAT
All specials unlocked and in player's special list	LOTSOFTRICKS
Full Stats	BEEFEDUP
Give player +50 skill points	NEEDSHELP
Unlocks Perfect Manual	STILLAINTFALLIN
Unlocks Perfect Rail	AINTFALLIN
Unlocks Unlimited Focus	MYOPIC
Invisible Man	THEMISSING
Mini Skater	TINYTATER

TRANSFORMERS: THE GAME

INFINITE HEALTH

At the Main menu, press Left, Left, Up, Left, Right, Down, Right.

INFINITE AMMO

At the Main menu, press Up, Down, Left, Right, Up, Up, Down.

NO MILITARY OR POLICE

At the Main menu, press Right, Left, Right, Left, Right, Left, Right.

ALL MISSIONS

At the Main menu, press Down, Up, Left, Right, Right, Right, Up, Down.

BONUS CYBERTRON MISSIONS

At the Main menu, press Right, Up, Up, Down, Right, Left, Left.

GENERATION 1 SKIN: JAZZ

At the Main menu, press Left, Up, Down, Down, Left, Up, Right.

GENERATION 1 SKIN: MEGATRON

At the Main menu, press Down, Left, Left, Down, Right, Right, Up.

GENERATION 1 SKIN: OPTIMUS PRIME

At the Main menu, press Down, Right, Left, Up, Down, Down, Left.

GENERATION 1 SKIN: ROBOVISION OPTIMUS PRIME

At the Main menu, press Down, Down, Up, Up, Right, Right, Right.

GENERATION 1 SKIN: STARSCREAM

At the Main menu, press Right, Down, Left, Left, Down, Up, Up.

ALL COVERS

Pause the game and select Controller Setup from the Options. Press Left, Left, Right, Left, Up, Left, Left, Down.

ALL CONCEPT ART

Pause the game and select Controller Setup from the Options. Press Down, Down, Down, Up, Down, Up, Left, Left.

ALL LANDMARKS

Pause the game and select Controller Setup from the Options. Press Up, Right, Down, Left, Down, Up, Right, Left.

UP

You will need to activate the following cheats at the pause menu after entering them.

RUSSELL ATTRACTS ALL BUTTERFLIES

Select Cheats from the Bonuses menu and enter BUTTERFLY.

MUNTZ'S AVIATOR GOGGLES FOR CARL

Select Cheats from the Bonuses menu and enter AVIATORGOGGLES.

CARL JUMPS FROM TEETER TOTTER TO LIFT RUSSEL

Select Cheats from the Bonuses menu and enter CARLHEAVYWEIGHT.

BALLOONS WHEN CARL JUMPS

Select Cheats from the Bonuses menu and enter BALLOONPARTY.

WWE SMACKDOWN VS. RAW 2009

BOOGEYMAN

Select Cheat Codes from My WWE and enter BoogeymanEatsWorms!!.

GENE SNITSKY

Select Cheat Codes from My WWE and enter UnlockSnitskySvR2009.

HAWKINS & RYDER

Select Cheat Codes from My WWE and enter Ryder&HawkinsTagTeam.

JILLIAN HALL

Select Cheat Codes from My WWE and enter PlayAsJillianHallSvR.

LAYLA

Select Cheat Codes from My WWE and enter UnlockECWDivaLayla09.

RIC FLAIR

Select Cheat Codes from My WWE and enter FlairWoooooooooooooo.

TAZZ

Select Cheat Codes from My WWE and enter UnlockECWTazzSvR2009.

VINCENT MCMAHON

Select Cheat Codes from My WWE and enter VinceMcMahonNoChance.

HORNSWOGGLE AS MANAGER

Select Cheat Codes from My WWE and enter HornswoggleAsManager.

CHRIS JERICHO COSTUME B

Select Cheat Codes from My WWE and enter AltJerichoModelSvR09.

CM PUNK COSTUME B

Select Cheat Codes from My WWE and enter CMPunkAltCostumeSvR!.

REY MYSTERIO COSTUME B

Select Cheat Codes from My WWE and enter BooyakaBooyaka619SvR.

SATURDAY NIGHT'S MAIN EVENT ARENA

Select Cheat Codes from My WWE and enter SatNightMainEventSvR.

WWE SMACKDOWN VS. RAW 2010

THE ROCK

Select Cheat Codes from the Options and enter The Great One.

VINCE'S OFFICE AND DIRT SHEET FOR BACKSTAGE BRAWL

Select Cheat Codes from the Options menu and enter BonusBrawl.

SHAWN MICHAELS' NEW COSTUME

Select Cheat Codes from the Options menu and enter Bow Down.

RANDY ORTON'S NEW COSTUME

Select Cheat Codes from the Options menu and enter ViperRKO.

TRIPLE H'S NEW COSTUME

Select Cheat Codes from the Options menu and enter Suck IT!.

X-MEN: THE OFFICIAL GAME

DANGER ROOM ICEMAN

At the Cerebro Files menu, press Right, Right, Left, Left, Down, Up, Down, Up, Start.

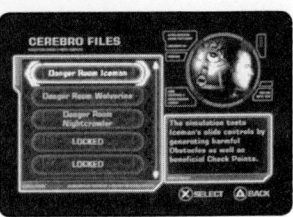

DANGER ROOM NIGHTCRAWLER

At the Cerebro Files menu, press Up, Up, Down, Down, Left, Right, Left, Right, Start.

DANGER ROOM WOLVERINE

At the Cerebro Files menu, press Down, Down, Up, Up, Right, Left, Right, Left, Start.